WRITE
FEARLESSLY!

WRITE FEARLESSLY!

Conquer Fear.
Eliminate Self-Doubt.
Write with Confidence.

Jim Denney

First eBook Edition: November 2013

First Trade Paper Edition: November 2013.

Cover design by The Wordsmith.

Visit the author's web site at
http://unearthlyfiction.wordpress.com/.

*To Fred Judkins,
whose life speaks volumes
about faith and courage*

About the Author

Jim Denney has more than a hundred published books to his credit, including the Timebenders science-fantasy series for young readers (*Battle Before Time*, *Doorway to Doom*, *Invasion of the Time Troopers*, and *Lost in Cydonia*). He has collaborated on books with numerous celebrities, including supermodel Kim Alexis, *Star Trek* actress Grace Lee Whitney, and two Super Bowl champions, quarterback Bob Griese and "The Minister of Defense," Reggie White. He has co-written many books with Pat Williams (co-founder of the Orlando Magic), including *Leadership Excellence* and *The Difference You Make*.

This book is 40,000 words in length, and was written using the principles in the author's previous book, *Writing in Overdrive: Write Faster, Write Freely, Write Brilliantly*, available in both ebook and trade paperback formats at Amazon.com. The author composed this book in first draft over a period of about twenty days, from September 14 to October 3, 2013. To learn how you can write brilliantly by writing quickly, read *Writing in Overdrive*.

Follow Jim Denney on Twitter at **@WriterJimDenney**. He blogs at http://unearthlyfiction.wordpress.com/.

Contents

Introduction   11
"Fear Is the Mind-Killer"

Fear No. 1   16
"I'm Afraid I Have No Talent"

Fear No. 2   30
"I'm Afraid to Begin"

Fear No. 3   43
"I'm Afraid I Can't Finish"

Fear No. 4   58
"I Fear the Risks of the Writer's Life"

Fear No. 5   77
"I'm Afraid to Reveal Who I Am"

Fear No. 6   100
"I'm Afraid of Rejection"

Fear No. 7   113
"I'm Afraid I Might Fail"

Fear No. 8   125
"I'm Afraid I Might Succeed"

Epilogue   136
"Be Invincible"

Recommended Reading   148

Recommended Software   152

WRITE
FEARLESSLY!

Introduction
"Fear Is the Mind-Killer"

———

"Fiction never exceeds the reach of the writer's courage."
Dorothy Alison

———

A few years into my career as a full-time writer, an editor called me. I had written several books for her in the past, and she liked my work.

"Jim," she said, "are you sitting down? I have a celebrity autobiography I want you to co-write, and you just won't believe who you'll be working with." She said the name of the celebrity — then waited for me to be wowed.

"Wow!" I said with 100 percent fake enthusiasm. "That's fantastic! When do I start?"

I had absolutely no clue who this celebrity was — but it had been a long time since my last paycheck and I needed the work.

As the editor explained the project to me, I felt a tingle of dread. I had never written a book like this before. I didn't know anything about this individual or the subject matter. I didn't know if I could pull it off — but I *had* to pull it off. I had a family to feed and a mortgage to pay. I took the job.

This was back in the days before Google, so research wasn't nearly as easy as it is today. But by the time I flew out to interview the celebrity, I was ready. I was able to ask hundreds of intelligent questions — and the celebrity was very impressed with my knowledge. It was a fascinating book to write, and having that book on my résumé helped me line up many more writing gigs.

The moral of the story: Take risks. Accept new challenges, even if you aren't sure you can pull it off. Every time you accept a challenge and attempt something you've never done before — *and you succeed* — your confidence grows. So step into the unknown and write fearlessly. That's how you build your confidence and overcome your fears.

In Frank Herbert's 1965 science fiction bestseller *Dune*, the hero, Paul Atreides, learns to control his fear by reciting the Litany Against Fear from the sacred rite of the Bene Gesserit religious sect:

> "I must not fear. Fear is the mind-killer. Fear is the little-death that brings total obliteration. I will face my fear. I will permit it to pass over me and through me. And when it has gone past I will turn the inner eye to see its path. Where the fear has gone there will be nothing. Only I will remain."[1]

There is enormous wisdom in those words. Fear is the mind-killer that obliterates our creativity and imagination. We cannot eliminate fear. In fact, fear has a beneficial role in our lives. Fear can paralyze us — but it can also alert us to danger and help keep us safe. That's why the Litany says, "I will face my fear. I will permit it to pass over me and through me."

Facing our fears makes us wiser and stronger. We must never allow fear, the mind-killer, to paralyze us or stampede us. We must control our fear through our courage. As people of courage, we acknowledge our fear, *but we refuse to let fear control us.*

Great writing is courageous writing. Any writing we produce in a state of fear will be self-conscious and shallow. If we fear the criticism of others, if we worry what readers and critics think of us, we'll be afraid to take creative risks and our writing will be contrived and inhibited. If we lack the courage to write honestly and vulnerably, our writing will be untruthful and unconvincing.

Have you ever read a piece of writing that was written out of fear? I have. I can sense it when a writer is playing it safe — self-censoring to avoid being criticized. I've read passages where I've said to myself, "I know what this author wanted to say, wanted to depict, wanted to have the characters do and say — but this author didn't dare go there."

I can smell fear on the page. I'm sure you can, too.

In *The War of Art*, Steven Pressfield identifies a struggle that takes place in every creative individual. He calls this struggle "Resistance," and he says that Resistance is often manifested as fear. He writes:

> Fear is good. ... Fear tells us what we have to do. ...
>
> The more scared we are of a work or calling, the more sure we can be that we have to do it.
>
> Resistance is experienced as fear; the degree of fear equates to the strength of Resistance. Therefore the more fear we feel about a specific enterprise, the more certain we can be that that enterprise is important to us and to the growth of our soul. That's why we feel so much Resistance. If it meant nothing to us, there'd be no Resistance. ...
>
> The professional tackles the project that will make him stretch. He takes on the assignment that will bear him into uncharted waters, compel him to explore

13

unconscious parts of himself.

So if you're paralyzed with fear, it's a good sign. It shows you what you have to do.[2]

As writers, we can't afford to be ruled by fear. Yes, we must *listen* to our fears, because our fears may be trying to tell us something important. But we mustn't run from our fears. *The thing we fear most is the thing we must do.* The story, scene, or moment of self-revelation that fills us with terror is the very truth we must write.

Anne Rice said, "If you're writing, you need courage, you need faith in yourself that's as strong as any talent you may possess." That's why I've written a book called *Write Fearlessly!* I've written this book to show you how to find the courage to match your talent.

I have spent more than twenty-five years as a professional writer, and I've studied this craft intensely. I've read scores of books on writing, and I've had countless conversations with fellow writers. As a result of my study, I've concluded that the number one factor that holds writers back is *fear.* We may call it anxiety or insecurity or self-doubt, but it really comes down to some sort of fear —

• The fear that we lack talent.

• The fear of the blank page, the fear of getting started.

• The fear that we cannot finish.

• The fear of the risks of the writer's life.

• The fear of exposing ourselves to the world through our writing.

• The fear of rejection.

• The fear of failure.

• And the most paradoxical fear of all, fear of success.

In this book, I'll take these fears apart and share with you the practical strategies you need to overcome each one. After reading this book, you'll find your confidence boosted and your motivation soaring. You'll feel inspired and empowered to write.

If fear has been holding you back as a writer, it's time you learned to write from your courage and confidence. It's time you learned to *write fearlessly.*

— Jim Denney

---

1. Frank Herbert, *Dune* (New York: Berkley, 2005), 8.
2. Steven Pressfield, *The War of Art: Break Through the Blocks and Win Your Inner Creative Battles* (New York: Warner, 2002), 40-41.

Fear No. 1
"I'm Afraid I Have No Talent"

―――――

"Whether or not you write well, write bravely."
Bill Stout

―――――

Anne Sexton was the prototype of the confessional poet. She wrote candidly about such themes as sexuality, abortion, addiction, and incest. She was also one of the most honored poets in America, winning the Pulitzer Prize in 1967, less than a dozen years after writing her first sonnet. Yet her fear nearly kept her from becoming a poet.

Diagnosed as bipolar when she was in her early twenties, Sexton was subject to depression and anxiety throughout her life. Her psychiatrist encouraged her to write poetry as a way of venting her feelings. When Sexton learned of an upcoming workshop conducted by the renowned poet John Holmes, she desperately wanted to attend — yet the thought of taking part in the workshop also terrified her. She feared exposing her poems to critiques from Holmes and from fellow students.

Unable to bring herself to register for the workshop, Anne Sexton asked a friend to register for her and to go with her to the first session. Soon after attending the workshop, Sexton began selling poems to some of the top magazines in the country, including *Harper's*, *The New Yorker*, and *Saturday Review*. She quickly became one of the most widely acclaimed poets in the world. But none of this acclaim would have come her way if she had not learned to master her fear.

The fear that afflicted Anne Sexton is common to most writers, though it is often expressed in different ways: "I'm afraid of letting other people read and critique my work," or, "I'm afraid I don't have what it takes to be a published author," or, "I'm afraid I have no talent." This fear is often referred to simply as *self-doubt*.

This fear afflicts writers on an epidemic scale. Self-doubt causes more suffering to writers than eyestrain, carpal tunnel syndrome, and writer's block combined. "The worst enemy to creativity is self-doubt," Sylvia Plath wrote in her journal during her student days at Smith College.

Self-doubt is the nagging, cruel voice in your head that says, "Why do you waste so many hours alone at this keyboard? You can't do this. No one will ever read what you write. You'll never be a published author. You're just fooling yourself."

Does this sound familiar? Am I describing the fear that holds *you* back? Are you afraid of finding out you don't have the talent to be a writer? Are you afraid of having your work seen and judged by others?

The voice of self-doubt can keep you from taking the risk of writing. And the tragic, ironic truth is that when you avoid the risk of writing, you risk everything. You risk your dreams. You risk your future. You risk the rewards of a lifetime. You risk your one and only irreplaceable self. As Erica Jong, author of *Witches*, once admitted:

I went for years not finishing anything. Because, of course, when you finish something you can be judged.

My poems used to go through 360 drafts. I had columns which were rewritten so many times that I suspect it was just a way of avoiding sending them out. ... When I look at some of those drafts, I realize that beyond a certain point I wasn't improving anything. I was obsessing. I was afraid to take risks.[1]

Speaking through one of her characters in her novel *How to Save Your Own Life*, Jong warns that when we allow fear to paralyze us, we risk throwing everything away. "The risk is your life," she wrote. "Wasting it, I mean. It's a pretty big risk. ... And the trouble is, if you don't risk anything, you risk even *more*. Life doesn't leave that many choices. It's really very harsh."[2]

How do you conquer the fear that you're not good enough? *You write.* You do the work. Even if you don't believe in yourself, even if you are fearful, even if you think your writing is so wretched that even your own mother would give it a one-star review on Amazon.com, you *write*.

Novelist Ayn Rand said that writers must adopt a mindset of relentless professionalism, regardless of self-doubts, in order to continue writing:

> The secret of writing is to be professional about it.
>
> You can be professional before you publish anything — *if* you approach writing as a job. If you apply to writing the same standards and methods that people regularly apply to other professions, you will take a lot of weight off your subconscious and increase your productive capacity.
>
> If you do not regard writing as a job, self-doubt will necessarily enter your mind, and you will be paralyzed. You will be putting yourself on trial every time you attempt to write. ... It will be a miracle if you

ever connect two sentences. ...

I regard the piece of paper as my employer. I have to fill that piece of paper. How I feel — whether it is difficult or not, whether I am stuck or not — is irrelevant. It is as irrelevant as it would be if I were an employee of Hank Rearden [the ruthless industrialist in her novel *Atlas Shrugged*]. He would not tolerate it if I told him, "I can't work today because I have self-doubt" or "I have a self-esteem crisis." Yet that is what most people do, in effect, when it comes to writing.[3]

One of the worst side-effects of fear is the loneliness it inflicts on us. We think we're the only ones who feel these fears. We picture our favorite authors, our literary heroes, the ones who make writing look so easy and effortless, and we think, "I wish I was fearless like him," or, "I wish I had her courage and self-confidence."

If you've ever had such thoughts, I have news for you. *All* writers experience self-doubt. Some manage to overcome their insecurities over time, but many extremely successful, multi-published authors wrestle with fear and self-doubt throughout their careers.

Detective fiction author Sara Paretsky is the creator of the hard-drinking, opera-loving woman private investigator V. I. Warshawski. Paretsky also co-founded Sisters in Crime and was named the 2011 Grand Master by Mystery Writers of America. With more than a dozen novels in print, you'd think she'd have nothing to fear as a writer, yet she once confessed, "Sometimes I panic and think I can't really write."

All writers, without exception, struggle with self-doubt. The great writers, the successful writers, are the ones who listen to their courage, not their doubts. They accept their fear, and keep writing anyway.

Unfortunately, many talented writers allow their fears to silence them. They possess a capacity for greatness, but can't bring themselves to express their dreams on the page. As the nineteenth-century English writer Sydney Smith observed, "A great deal of talent is lost to the world for want of a little courage." Don't let your talent be lost to the world. Write fearlessly by applying these principles:

1. Write fast enough to stay ahead of your doubts.

Horror master Stephen King observed, "Writing fiction, especially a long work of fiction, can be a difficult, lonely job. It's like crossing the Atlantic Ocean in a bathtub. There is plenty of opportunity for self-doubt." King's solution: *Write quickly.* He explains:

> With the door shut, downloading what's in my head directly to the page, I write as fast as I can and still remain comfortable. ... If I write rapidly, putting down my story exactly as it comes into my mind ... I find that I can keep up with my original enthusiasm and at the same time outrun the self-doubt that's always waiting to settle in.[4]

Detective fiction writer Raymond Chandler put it this way: "The faster I write the better my output. If I'm going slow, I'm in trouble. It means I'm pushing the words instead of being pulled by them."

So the first step in eliminating self-doubt is to write fast enough to stay ahead of your doubts. Don't stop to edit, do research, or dawdle lazily over your page. If you pause for even a moment, your doubts may catch up to you. So don't hesitate, don't look back — keep writing! And write quickly.

2. Put an end to perfectionism

Some writers have an obsessive-compulsive need to polish and perfect each sentence before moving on to the next. All obsessive-compulsive perfectionist tendencies are rooted in fear. Perfectionists fear that someone might see one of their first-draft sentences and judge them for their imperfection. They are unable to simply write and have fun with words. They are tormented by the obsessive, dysfunctional demands of their perfectionism.

They type a sentence — and immediately begin editing that sentence. They fuss over it and fiddle with it until they're sure it's perfect. Then, reluctantly, they type another sentence, and they edit that. Another sentence, another edit. And after an incredibly long time, they have assembled row upon row of neat little sentences, each one individually sculpted and painstakingly perfected.

But as you read through those sentences, there is no flow to them. The writing is passionless, stiff, and self-conscious. The words are lifeless and just lie there on the page without any sense of rhythm and exhilaration. Why? Because when you write from your fear and your obsessive-compulsive perfectionism, you are writing from your critical and analytical intellect, not from your uninhibited imagination, your Muse, your soul.

If you want to write brilliantly, you must put an end to perfectionism. You must shed your obsessive-compulsive urge to clean up after each sentence. Give yourself permission to make a beautiful, creative, uninhibited mess — and you'll write brilliantly, passionately, and fearlessly. Anne Lamott put it this way in *Bird by Bird*:

> Perfectionism is the voice of the oppressor, the enemy of the people. It will keep you cramped and

insane your whole life. ... Perfectionism is based on the obsessive belief that if you run carefully enough, hitting each stepping-stone just right, you won't have to die. The truth is that you will die anyway. ...

Perfectionism will ruin your writing, blocking inventiveness and playfulness. ... Perfectionism means that you try desperately not to leave so much mess to clean up. But clutter and mess show us that life is being lived. Clutter is wonderfully fertile ground.[5]

So loosen up! Have fun! Give yourself permission to write badly. Play with your words like a child playing with her Cheerios. Write a fast, messy, exuberant first draft. Sure, it will be filled with typos and grammatical errors and bad sentences — but you'll clean it all up in rewrite. The most important task of writing in first draft is to capture lightning on the page, to be passionate and joyfully imperfect.

Giving yourself permission to write badly is one of the keys to writing brilliantly and fearlessly.

3. Don't beat yourself up or talk yourself down.

Be your own best encourager. Keep telling yourself, "I can do this." Don't get a swelled head. Don't get down on yourself. Keep an even keel.

Gail Carson Levine writes young adult fantasy novels such as *Ella Enchanted*, which received a Newbery Honor in 1998. She is noted for retelling classic fairy tales for today's readers. "Do not beat up on yourself," she says. "Do not criticize your writing as lousy, inadequate, stupid, or any of the evil epithets that you are used to heaping on yourself. Such self-bashing is never useful. If you indulge in it, your writing doesn't stand a chance. So when your mind turns on you, turn it back, stamp it down, shut it up, and keep writing."[6]

Freelance fiction editor and novel doctor Stephen Parolini has worked with some of the top novelists in the business, including Ted Dekker, Kristen Heitzmann, and Tosca Lee. He observes: "Writers are notorious self-talkers. We have to be. All of our employees live in our head. Self-talk is our way of motivating them to do their jobs. But not all our self-talk is helping. ... Negativity (and also just plain wrongful thinking) leaves a residue that can poison your writing life."

Parolini notes that even some of what we might call "positive" self-talk can actually have a negative impact on our writing. Those who tell themselves, "I'm going to write a bestseller" or "I'm going to be the next J.K. Rowling" are setting themselves up for disappointment and depression if they fail to achieve that lofty goal. Instead, Parolini says, tell yourself, "I'm going to write the best damn book I can."

Avoid extreme self-talk, Parolini says, such as "I'm brilliant" or "I suck as a writer." Instead, tell yourself, "I have a long way to go as a writer." Every writer has much to learn. As Hemingway once said, "We are all apprentices in a craft where no one ever becomes a master."

Finally, Parolini warns that we should not say, "I'm ten times a better writer than [insert bestselling author here]." Such a statement, he says, is a "dangerous motivator." It might propel you for a while, but it doesn't produce long-term healthy results. If you were to say such words out loud in front of other people, they'd think you are smug, delusional, and narcissistic. And if you never achieve the acclaim and sales figures of [insert bestselling author here], you set yourself up for disappointment and bitterness.

Instead of comparing ourselves to other writers, Parolini says, we should simply say, "I am a writer." He concludes: "Those four words are magic. Say them often. ... 'I am a writer.' Say it again. 'I am a writer.' Yes. You are. So write."[7]

4. Write daily, whether you feel like it or not.

John Steinbeck battled self-doubt while writing *The Grapes of Wrath*, even though he had been a successful author for nearly a decade, having published six previous novels and two story collections. In a journal entry for August 16, 1938, midway through his first draft of *The Grapes of Wrath*, he wrote: "I should really not try to write books in the summer. ... I feel like letting everything go. ... My many weaknesses are beginning to show their heads. ... I'm not a writer. I've been fooling myself."

If Steinbeck felt that way, then who is immune to such fears? After recording his doubts in his journal, he turned a deaf ear to them, adding, "I'll try to go on with work now. Just a stint every day does it."[8]

The book he was writing at the time, the novel that made him say "I'm not a writer," is the same novel that won the Pulitzer Prize and helped secure the Nobel Prize for Literature. So if your doubts are telling you you're not a writer, you just might be in for a life-changing surprise.

Another Pulitzer-winning writer of fiction and nonfiction, Richard Rhodes, offers this advice to writers who struggle with fear and self-doubt:

> If you're afraid you can't write, the answer is to write. Every sentence you construct adds weight to the balance pan. If you're afraid of what other people will think of your efforts, don't show them until you write your way beyond your fear. If writing a book is impossible, write a chapter. If writing a chapter is impossible, write a page. If writing a page is impossible, write a paragraph. If writing a paragraph is impossible, write a sentence. If writing even a sentence is impossible, write a word and teach

yourself everything there is to know about that word and then write another connected word and see where their connection leads. A page a day is a book a year.[9]

So get on with your daily work. Just a stint every day does it. Whether you feel like it or not, *write*.

5. Write confidently by writing in the zone.

Great fiction writing is not primarily an act of the intellect but the product of a creative state called being "in flow" or "in the zone." This experience is much like self-hypnosis. When you write "in the zone," you experience a passionate, emotional involvement in your work combined with intense concentration and a state of relaxation. Your creative energies are at their peak, and you feel uninhibited and free to enter an experience of pure imagination.

The ancient Greeks and Romans were well aware of this state. The Greeks identified the "zone" with the activity of goddesses of inspiration called "the Muses." The Romans referred to this state as *furor poeticus*, the poetic frenzy.

Lu Chi (A.D. 261-303), a Chinese poet and philosopher during the Three Kingdoms period, also wrote about the "in the zone" experience in his *Wen Fu* (*Rhyme-Prose On Literature*). He wrote that the writer in the grip of this experience "floats on the heavenly lake; he steeps himself in the nether spring. Thereupon, submerged words squirm up, as when a flashing fish, hook in its gills, leaps from water's depth. ... He gathers words untouched by a hundred generations; he plucks rhythms unsung for a thousand years. He sees past and present in a moment; he reaches for the four seas in the twinkling of an eye."[10]

From the ancient Greeks, Romans, and Chinese to such writers as Ray Bradbury, Anne Lamott, Stephen King, and

Ursula Le Guin, descriptions of the "zone" are remarkably similar, and are always marked by emotions of joy that cancel out fear. Ursula Le Guin describes her writing process as "a pure trance state. ... All I seek when writing is to allow my unconscious mind to control the course of the story, using rational thought only to reality check when revising."[11]

The person in "flow" loses self-awareness and seems to merge with the writing process. Writing becomes spontaneous, and the words, images, and metaphors seem to come from outside oneself. The writer is able to focus totally on the work, blocking out all distractions. In this state, the writer feels masterful and in control, yet also feels mastered and controlled by the work itself. The writer's fictional characters seem to come alive and take on a life of their own.

One of the most intriguing features of the "in the zone" experience is that the passage of time becomes an elastic experience. Hours can seem to pass in minutes, and minutes can seem to expand into hours. In "the zone" we are shut off from the external distractions of the outside world and the internal distractions of our mental chatter. We do not think analytically. We are immersed in the dreamlike state of the creative act.

By shutting off our mental noise, we silence the voice of our fears. While writing "in the zone," we experience no self-doubt, no self-criticism, no self-awareness at all. We are not worried about whether our writing is good or not, whether we have talent or not, whether we can finish or not, whether editors and readers will like our work or not, or whether we will succeed or fail. All that matters "in the zone" is the story, the characters, the images, the work.

In "the zone," we becomes fearless. As Susan Johnson describes in her novel *A Better Woman*, "In my writing life I was totally fearless and everything cloudy was magically rendered transparent. I was intoxicated by writing."[12]

[**Author's Note:** I discuss practical techniques for tapping into the unconscious mind and writing "in the zone" in my book *Writing in Overdrive: Write Faster, Write Freely, Write Brilliantly.* — J.D.]

6. Whether you write well or write badly, *just write.*

The only way to learn writing is by writing. Susan Sontag said, "By writing much one learns to write well." The only way to improve is to write and write and write. Practice and persistence are much more important than so-called "natural talent." A lot of people who appear "naturally talented" have simply put the time and practice in, driving themselves to keep writing even though they suffered from the same fears and doubts you feel right now.

Before Canadian-born writer David Rakoff died in 2012 at age forty-seven, he left this wise insight to us:

> I have so little control over the act of writing that it's all I can do to remain conscious. Actual formal considerations are almost beyond my capacity. Before I sat down and became a writer, before I began to do it habitually and for my living, there was a decades-long stretch when I was terrified that it would suck, so I didn't write. I think that marks a lot of people, a real terror at being bad at something, and unfortunately you are always bad before you can get a little better.[13]

When you write, don't worry about whether or not you have talent. There are many talented people who will never accomplish anything because they lack the courage to write. And there are people of modest talent who have set the literary world on fire through their courageous writing.

27

If you didn't have the courage to be a writer, you wouldn't be reading these words right now. You'd be making excuses for not writing. But here you are, mustering your courage and looking for that one little motivational nudge to get you going.

Well, here's that nudge, courtesy of novelist Jessamyn West, author of *The Friendly Persuasion*: "Talent is helpful in writing, but guts are absolutely essential."

I believe you've got the guts. Prove me right. *Start writing.*

---

1. Charlotte Templin, ed., *Conversations With Erica Jong* (Jackson MS: University Press of Mississippi, 2002), 12.

2. Erica Jong, *How to Save Your Own Life* (New York: Tarcher, 2006), 263.

3. Ayn Rand, *The Art of Nonfiction: A Guide for Writers and Readers* (New York: Penguin, 2001), 3-4.

4. Stephen King, *On Writing: A Memoir of the Craft* (10th Anniversary Edition: New York: Pocket Books, 2000), 210.

5. Anne Lamott, *Bird by Bird: Some Instructions on Writing and Life* (New York: Anchor, 1995), 28.

6. Rebecca D. Monaco, "In the Words of Gail Carson Levine," Goodreads.com, August 3, 2011, http://www.goodreads.com/author_blog_posts/1488063-in-the-words-of-gail-carson-levine.

7. Stephen Parolini, "Self-Talk for Writers," NovelDoctor.com, September 23, 2012, http://www.noveldoctor.com/2012/09/23/self-talk-for-writers/.

8. John Steinbeck, Robert DeMott, ed., *Working Days: The Journals of The Grapes of Wrath, 1938-1941* (New York: Penguin, 1990), Kindle edition, Entry #52, August 16, 1938.

9. Richard Rhodes, *How to Write: Advice and Reflections* (New York: HarperCollins, 2009), Kindle edition.

10. Lu Chi, *Rhyme-Prose On Literature (Wen Fu)*, translated by Achilles Fang, *The New Directions Anthology of Classical Chinese Poetry*, edited by Eliot Weinberger (New York: New Directions, 2003), 184.

11. Ursula K. Le Guin, "A Reponse, by Ansible, from Tau Ceti," in Laurence Davis and Peter Stillman, eds., *The New Utopian Politics of*

Ursula K. Le Guin's The Dispossessed (Lanham: Rowman and Littlefield. 2005), 305.

12. Susan Johnson, *A Better Woman: A Memoir of Motherhood* (New York: Washington Square, 1999), 86.

13. John Winokur, "You Are Always Bad Before You Can Get a Little Better," AdviceToWriters.com, November 25, 2012, http://www.advicetowriters.com/home/2012/11/25/you-are-always-bad-before-you-can-get-a-little-better.html.

Fear No. 2
"I'm Afraid to Begin"

———

"The scariest moment is always just before you start ."
Stephen King

———

I once taught a writer's workshop and a young woman came to me after a session and said, "I just can't get started. I know what I want to write about, and I know my characters — it all seems so perfect in my head. But when I try to write the perfect opening line, nothing comes to me — nothing that feels good enough. Without a brilliant first sentence, I can't write the rest of the story. I'm afraid to start writing."

This is a classic writer's fear — the fear of the blank page (or the blank screen). Most writers overcome this fear with experience. But a surprising number of experienced writers continue to be afflicted with fear of the blank page well into their careers.

Margaret Atwood, author of *The Handmaid's Tale*, has won many literary awards, including the prestigious Booker Prize. Yet even after publishing more than a dozen novels, plus story collections, poetry collections, and children's books, she still says, "Blank pages inspire me with terror."

Oscar- and Emmy-winning screenwriter/producer Aaron Sorkin (*The West Wing, The Social Network*) says, "I love writing, but hate starting. The page is awfully white and it says, 'You may have fooled some of the people some of the time but those days are over. ... I'm a white piece of paper. You wanna dance with me?' And I really, really don't."[1]

Before Colombian novelist Gabriel García Márquez could sell 30 million copies of *One Hundred Years of Solitude* and collect the Nobel Prize for Literature, he had to work up the courage to write the first line. "All my life," Márquez once told an interviewer, "I've been frightened at the moment I sit down to write. ... Terribly frightened."[2]

And another Nobel winner, John Steinbeck, wrote in his journal, "I suffer as always from the fear of putting down the first line. It is amazing the terrors, the magics, the prayers, the straightening shyness that assails one. ... A strange and mystic business, writing."[3]

The fear of the blank page may be as old as literature itself. In 1295, the poet Dante Alighieri wrote in *Vita Nuova* (*The New Life*), "It seemed to me that I had undertaken a theme too lofty for myself, so that I did not dare to begin writing, and I remained for several days with the desire to write and the fear of beginning."[4]

So if you struggle with fear of the blank page, you're in excellent company — and you don't have to be paralyzed by this fear. You can overcome it. Here are the practical tools to help you dispel this fear so you can write fearlessly:

1. Save the first for last.

A lot of well-meaning writing teachers do their students a disservice by teaching them, "You've got to rivet your reader's attention with a knockout first sentence." Yes, it's true that you need to grab the reader's attention very quickly, and certainly before the end of the first paragraph. But what writing teachers often fail to tell their students is that a book does *not* need to be written in the same order it will be read.

You can start writing in the middle, or somewhere near the end, or you can let the whole thing grow organically from a pile of tangled nouns and verbs. You don't have to write the first sentence before you write the second, and the second before the third, and so on.

Ray Bradbury's *Fahrenheit 451* had its beginnings as a 1947 short story called "Bright Phoenix." Bradbury expanded it into a 25,000-word novella, "The Fireman," in 1950. Neither of these early versions contains the signature opening line of the final novel: "It was a pleasure to burn." Only when Bradbury wrote the final 50,000-word novel did that opening line occur to him. The brilliant first line of *Fahrenheit 451* was one of the last sentences Bradbury wrote for the novel.

Sometime it's best to save the first for last.

When you face the blank page, forget trying to write the perfect first sentence. Forget perfectionism altogether. Don't listen to the voice of your Inner Critic or the voice of your old writing teacher. Just find any old way into the story and start writing. You might even put this down as the first sentence of your novel: [BRILLIANT OPENING SENTENCE GOES HERE.] Then keep writing the rest of your wonderful book.

Dorothea Brande, in *Becoming a Writer*, advises, "Simply start working. If a good first sentence does not come, leave a space for it and write it in later. Write as rapidly as possible."[5]

As you approach the blank page, your job is capture ideas out of the air and pin them to the page. Ideas are messy. Creativity is wild, exuberant fun. So have fun with ideas. When it's time to write your perfect opening line, it will come to you — probably with very little effort. And when it comes to you, you'll know it's right.

After your first draft is written, you'll know your story inside and out, backward and forward. Knowing your story can be a huge advantage in crafting a brilliant opening line. So be patient. Just write.

2. Refuse to let fear control you.

Approach the blank page with a chip on your shoulder. Tell fear to get off your back and out of your way. Refuse to let fear have its way with you. Erica Jong says that refusing to be controlled by fear is one of the greatest lessons life has taught her:

> All the good things that have happened to me in the last several years have come, without exception, from a willingness to change, to risk the unknown, to do the very things I feared most. Every poem, every page of fiction I have written, has been written with anxiety, occasionally panic, always uncertainty about its reception. Every life decision I have made — from changing jobs, to changing partners, to changing homes — has been taken with trepidation. I have not ceased being fearful, but I have ceased to let fear control me.[6]

One of the best ways I know to get fear out of your way is to *get mad at fear.* Despise it and abhor it. Snub it and spurn it. The greater your anger, the less your fear — and anger can be a great motivator to get you writing. Romance writer Jo Leigh (*One Wicked Night, Relentless*) has a simple, blunt maxim for dealing with fear of the blank page: "Screw the fear."

Nancy Slonim Aronie, an NPR commentator and author of *Writing from the Heart*, finds that her fear of the blank page comes from ego — a pride-centered fear that the first line in her first draft won't be brilliant. She writes:

This is about my fear — fear of starting out not great. How can I write garbage?

But were Flannery O'Connor's first lines, first attempts, first drafts brilliant? I doubt it.

I know it's only when my ego gets lodged between my heart and my work that it presents a problem. ... The main thing I always have to remember is that my ego doesn't have my best interests at heart. It wants the Oscar. But it doesn't care a bit about my soul.[7]

Don't let fear bully you, control your decisions, or frighten you away from the blank page. Take charge of your fear. Stare it down and show it who's boss. As dystopian novelist Tahereh Mafi wisely said, "The words get easier the moment you stop fearing them."

3. If you can't start writing, do writing-related tasks.

Now we come to treacherous territory.

Doing so-called "writing-related tasks" can easily become an excuse for procrastination. Getting on Google and doing "research" can become a way of putting off getting started, while telling ourselves it's really "writing-related." So I hesitate to advise you to try something that may actually keep you from writing.

At same time, I know you can often get unstuck by circling around your writing, probing and testing until you find a way in. To make sure you are truly approaching the blank page from a new angle, not simply avoiding it, set a time limit — no more than ten minutes — to do research, outlining, or note-making. Within those ten minutes, probably much sooner, a piece of information you turn up or a phrase you jot down will spark an idea — and you'll be off and writing.

Ray Bradbury often wandered among the stacks of the Los Angeles Main Library, trawling for inspiration and ideas. He'd take down a book, read a few lines of poetry or a paragraph from an astronomy book — and his brain cells would light up. He'd snatch a few slips of library scratch paper and a stubby little pencil, and he'd fill those slips of paper with notes and ideas. Then he'd hurry home and turn those ideas into stories.

Have you ever locked yourself out of your house? The front door clicks shut, you reach for your keys — and you remember you left them on the dining room table of your empty house. You stand and stare at the front door like some forlorn writer staring at a blank page. How will you get into that house? You check under the flower pot for the spare key — then remember you hung it on the kitchen wall, planning to put it back under the pot. You start circling around the house, looking for a way in. You rattle the back door. You mentally compare the width of the doggie door to your hips before deciding that's a non-starter. You check the bedroom windows, all locked shut. You check the bathroom window — and it opens! You have a way in!

And so it is, sometimes, with your story. You have to keep circling around and around your story, testing here, rattling there, measuring this or that, until you find an unlocked entryway. Young adult fantasy author Laini Taylor (*Daughter of Smoke and Bone*) says:

> Never sit staring at a blank page or screen. If you find yourself stuck, write. Write *about* the scene you're trying to write. *Writing about* is easier than *writing*, and chances are, it will give you your way in. You could try listing ten things that might happen next, or do a timed free-write — fast, non-precious forward momentum; you don't even have to read it afterward, but it might give you ideas. Try anything and everything. Never fall

still, and don't be lazy.[8]

Great advice. Keep writing, keep moving, keep pushing forward until you find a way into your story or novel. Once you are in, don't stop. Write on.

4. Try some writing "warm-up" exercises.

You might find inspiration by thinking about the book or story you want to write, then condensing its central idea into a single theme sentence. Often, clarifying the core idea of your story or novel can spark an idea for your opening page.

Instead of trying to write in complete sentences, jot down keywords that relate to your story, theme, or characters. Make lists of words. Once your paper or screen is no longer blank, your fear of the blank page should dissipate.

Write descriptions of your characters. Or interview your characters — ask them questions and record their responses. Your unconscious mind, speaking through your characters, might give you the perfect opening for your story.

Take paper and pen and start doodling with words and characters. Just play and have fun with your ideas. Doodling, drawing, and word-play is relaxing — and a relaxed mind is open to flashes of insight from the Muse, the unconscious mind. As soon as you start putting words and thoughts on paper, or start typing words onto your computer screen, you'll feel your mental logjam begin to break up. Ideas and words will flow — and you'll be writing again.

5. Don't try too hard.

Good writing is not something we *try* to do. It's something we *do*. Good writing flows naturally. The harder we try to write, the harder writing becomes.

Sometimes, we find it difficult to begin because we put too much pressure on ourselves. We're trying too hard to be clever or artsy. Or we're trying to impress. Or we're putting pressure on ourselves to be productive because we've got a word-count goal to reach.

When we realize we're trying too hard, the solution is to relax. That doesn't mean we stop writing. It doesn't mean we take the day off. It means we stop pressuring ourselves and simply write to have fun. Great writing is relaxed writing. You can be serious and be relaxed. You can work hard, our after hour, and still be emotionally and mentally relaxed.

Forcing your writing, putting pressure on yourself, telling yourself to try harder and write faster will not produce great writing. Ease up on yourself. Set aside your drivenness and perfectionism.

If you need ideas, step away from your keyboard, take a walk, take a shower, lie down and daydream, fix yourself a hot drink, or listen to music. Create a little space between yourself and your work — and allow your unconscious mind to fill that space with images, scenes, characters, and dialogue.

Don't stay away from the keyboard too long. Don't read or turn on the news or talk on the phone. Don't do anything that would fill that space with someone else's words. Don't play an addictive game on your computer or phone. Relax quietly. Ten or twenty minutes will do. When you come back to the keyboard, you'll be renewed and refreshed — and you'll probably have some powerful new ideas, ready to write.

Novelist Jennifer Gilmore (*Golden Country*) makes a serious point when she says, "What is it about the blank page that makes me want to hurl myself into a game of solitaire? I ask myself these kinds of questions while I'm playing solitaire."

So depressurize. Relax and don't try so hard. Have fun — and just write.

6. Make sure you are writing what you love to write.

Sometimes we find ourselves paralyzed in front of the blank page because we're trying to write something we don't love, something we really don't want to write about. That's when our unconscious mind rebels. That's when the Muse stamps off in a huff.

In order to write freely, we have to write what we love. If you write what you hate, your readers will hate it, too.

Ray Bradbury said, "Fall in love and stay in love. Write only what you love, and love what you write. The key word is love. You have to get up in the morning and write something you love, something to live for."

When you write what you love and love what you write, the blank page doesn't represent fear — it represents *freedom*, the freedom to dream, the freedom to invent entire worlds out of nothing. As the French philosopher Gaston Bachelard wrote in *The Poetics of Reverie*, "How can one not dream while writing? It is the pen which dreams. The blank page gives the right to dream. If only one could write for himself alone."[9]

And bestselling Scots novelist Irvine Welsh (*Trainspotting*) expressed this liberating view of the blank page:

> When people start writing there is this [mistaken] idea that you have to get everything right the first time, every sentence has to be perfect, every paragraph has to be perfect, every chapter has to be perfect. But what you're doing is not any kind of public show, until you're ready for it. There is a kind of mysticism to writing. ... I enjoy the freedom of the blank page.[10]

When you're in love with your characters, your idea, your story, the grand vision of the tale in your imagination, you'll sit down to the blank page and write brilliantly. Revel in the freedom of the blank page. Love is the key. "There is no fear in love," wrote St. John, "but perfect love drives out fear."[11]

7. Be afraid, and write anyway.

"It's the job that's never started as takes longest to finish," said Samwise Gamgee (quoting his Old Gaffer) in J. R. R. Tolkien's *The Fellowship of the Ring*. So accept your fear *and get started*. Go ahead and be afraid — *but write anyway.*

So you're afraid of the blank page. So what? What can the blank page do to you? How can it hurt you? What do you have to lose by throwing some words — any words — onto that glowing screen, that blank page?

You can rearrange those words, play with them, do some word association, let one word lead to another, and before you know it, you'll be writing. And your worst day of writing beats your best day of procrastinating, so you might as well write. As science fiction writer A. Lee Martinez observed, "Those who write are writers. Those who wait are waiters."

It takes courage to be a writer. Not a lot of courage, not the kind of physical courage it takes to be a cop or a firefighter or a member of the military. But it does take a certain kind of courage that is uncommon in the general population.

Anthony J. W. Benson, founder of Injoi Creative and Deeper Well Publishing, said, "Writers are a courageous lot. Often embattled by confusion, distraction and persistent dissatisfaction, they fight through pain, sweat and tears, as well as the unforgiving blinding glare of the blank page, to bring their thoughts forth."[12]

Courage, of course, is not the absence of fear. Rather, it's a determined, deliberate response to fear that says, "I'm afraid, but I won't let my fear stop me or control me. By the force of my will, I will do the thing I fear."

There are more than fourteen million copies of Jodi Picoult's twenty novels in print. And here's a fun fact: Did you know that Picoult also scripted five issues of DC Comics *Wonder Woman* in 2007? She has accomplished so much as a writer because she does not let fear of the blank page stop her from writing. "You might not write well every day," she once said, "but you can always edit a bad page. You can't edit a blank page."

8. Pray.

Writing is one of the most paradoxical of human activities. When you approach it the right way, writing is exuberant good fun. I like to call writing "finger-painting with words," to underscore my belief that great writing must be messy, uninhibited, and playful.

But here's the paradoxical part: Even when writing is fun, it's serious business. It's important. It's enduring. It's art. Let's not get pretentious about it, but writing *is* a creative endeavor. As Stephen King said, "You can approach the act of writing with nervousness, excitement, hopefulness, or even despair — the sense that you can never completely put on the page what's in your mind and heart. ... [But] you must not come lightly to the blank page."[13]

When I began writing this book, I did not come lightly to the blank page. I came with an awareness of a responsibility I have to you, my fellow writer. I know that if you are reading these words right now, you're struggling with real fears that are holding you back from reaching your full potential. So when I began planning this book, I approached it with prayer — a prayer that I would be inspired with the ideas and insights that would touch the fears you face. And I prayed for you, the reader, that you would find powerful encouragement and inspiration to meet your need as a writer.

I don't come lightly to this book. I come to it in an attitude of prayer. I come to it believing that the One who created the universe is also the One who ignites the spark of creativity within each of us. And I believe prayer is how we connect our creative human souls with the soul of the Creator.

Anne Lamott, in *Bird by Bird*, says she makes prayer her writing ritual as well as her spiritual discipline. Prayer is the means by which she gathers her courage to confront the blank page. "I sit for a moment," she writes, "and then say a small prayer — 'please help me get out of the way so I can write what wants to be written.' Sometimes ritual quiets the racket. Try it."[14]

What should you pray for? Pray for courage, inspiration, and ideas. Pray for wisdom. Pray for an opening line. Pray for the determination and imagination to continue writing, even if a brilliant opening line doesn't come to you.

Writing is wordplay and it's serious business. Pray — then play. Rejoice — then get down to business. Relax — then get to work. Face your fear — then write from your courage.

---

1. Melissa Crawley, *Mr. Sorkin Goes to Washington: Shaping the President on Television's The West Wing* (Jefferson, NC: McFarland & Co., 2006), 61.

2. Gene H. Bell-Villada, ed., *Conversations With Gabriel García Márquez* (Jackson MS: University Press of Mississippi, 2006), 147.

3. John Steinbeck, *Journal of a Novel: The East of Eden Letters* (New York: Penguin, 1990), Kindle edition, Entry for February 13, 1951.

4. Dante Alighieri, *Vita Nuova* (1295), in *The Portable Dante* (New York: Penguin, 2003), 610.

5. Dorothea Brande, *Becoming a Writer* (New York: Tarcher, 1981), 142.

6. Erica Jong, *What Do Women Want? Essays by Erica Jong* (New York: Tarcher, 2007), 62.

7. Nancy Slonim Aronie, *Writing from the Heart: Tapping the Power of Your Inner Voice* (New York: Hyperion, 1998), 119.

8. Laini Taylor, "Five Writing Tips from Laini Taylor," PublishersWeekly.com, November 16, 2012, http://www.publishersweekly.com/pw/by-topic/childrens/childrens-authors/article/54760-5-writing-tips-from-laini-taylor.html.

9. Gaston Bachelard, *The Poetics of Reverie: Childhood, Language, and the Cosmos* (Boston: Beacon Press, 1971), 17.

10. Irvine Welsh, "Literary Sparring: Alan Black interviews Irvine Welsh," *3am Magazine*, February 2004, http://www.3ammagazine.com/litarchives/2004/feb/interview_irvine_welsh.html.

11. 1 John 4:18a, New International Version.

12. Anthony J. W. Benson, "Writers Are a Courageous Lot," Facebook.com, November 20, 2012, https://www.facebook.com/notes/deeper-well-publishing/writers-are-a-courageous-lot/552023294812064.

13. Stephen King, *On Writing: A Memoir of the Craft* (10th Anniversary Edition: New York: Pocket Books, 2000), 99.

14. Anne Lamott, *Bird by Bird: Some Instructions on Writing and Life* (New York: Anchor, 1995), 117.

Fear No. 3
"I'm Afraid I Can't Finish"

———

"A writer is someone who finishes."
Thomas Farber

———

Ralph Ellison began writing his novel *Invisible Man* in early 1945. It's the story of an unnamed African-American man who lives in Depression-era New York City. The narrator describes himself as "invisible" because the culture around him refuses to acknowledge his existence.

He first-drafted the text in longhand and his wife Fanny assisted him in typing and editing the manuscript. After nearly seven years of work, Ellison completed the novel and sold it to Random House. Published in 1952, *Invisible Man* was praised by reviewers and quickly became an instant best-seller. It won the National Book Award for Fiction in 1953 (beating Ernest Hemingway's *The Old Man and the Sea*).

Ellison became one of the most highly regarded authors in the world, and *Invisible Man* became required reading in many high school and university courses. The literary world eagerly awaited his next novel, and over the next few years, several literary magazines published excerpts from a second novel-

43

length work that Ellison said was nearly finished. By the mid-1960s, however, it was becoming clear that Ellison's second novel was an endless project, a tale in search of an ending.

In November 1967, Ellison spent the morning working on the novel at his summer home in the Berkshires. After lunch, he and his wife Fanny left the house for a brief shopping trip. They returned to find the house engulfed in flames. Inside the burning home was the only copy of a 362-page section of his new novel.

By 1980, Ellison's second novel was still unpublished. When an interviewer asked him about the material lost in the fire, he said, "I guess I've been able to put most of it back together again."[1]

Though Ellison produced two volumes of essays, one in 1964 and another in 1986, Ellison said little about progress on his second novel. Many in the literary community speculated that Ellison was not seriously working on the novel or that he was blocked and unable to write. That speculation was wildly untrue.

At the time of Ellison's death in 1994, John F. Callahan, the executor of Ellison's literary estate, found more than 2,000 manuscript pages in Ellison's home — one incredibly long novel that Ellison was never able to bring to a conclusion. Callahan condensed a portion of the 2,000-page manuscript to a 368-page stand-alone novel, then published it in 1999 under the title *Juneteenth*. He condensed the rest of the manuscript to a still-unwieldy 1,101-page book called *Three Days Before the Shooting...*, published in 2010.

Ralph Ellison spent more than forty years on a "second novel" that he never finished. Critics concluded that the two books Callahan carved out of Ellison's unfinished manuscript failed to fulfill the promise of *Invisible Man*. Some critics believed Ellison was never able to recapture the unique "voice" of his original novel. Others believed that Ellison's first novel garnered so much acclaim, so much praise, that the pressure to compete with himself was too great. He had a lofty vision of what he wanted his next novel to be, and it was a vision no novelist could live up to.

So for forty years, until his death, Ralph Ellison lived with a gnawing fear: "What if I can't finish?"

Endlessly driven or hopelessly blocked?

This fear, "I'm afraid I can't finish," is one of the most common and haunting fears writers suffer. As you'd expect, it is epidemic among aspiring, unpublished writers — yet it's surprisingly common among writers who are successfully published and highly acclaimed. In some cases, as with Ralph Ellison, this fear may drive a writer to work endlessly on a single project, producing countless pages but no conclusion.

In other writers, this fear can take the form of a lengthy writer's block, in which the writer is unable to work on the novel at all. The writer who has never written a novel before may lack the confidence that he or she can go the distance: "I don't know how to begin. I'm not sure I can sustain the middle. I doubt I can write a worthy ending. I'm defeated before I begin."

Even multi-published authors often build up a mental vision of their novel that is so grand and glorious than it actually becomes intimidating and self-defeating. We say to ourselves, "The novel I picture in my mind is so rich in theme, so vast in scope, that I don't feel capable of writing it. I'd better wait until I acquire the skills to do it justice."

These are the same fears Ray Bradbury faced in January 1953 when he signed a contract to expand his 25,000-word novella "The Fireman" to novel length. A short story writer, Bradbury had never written a novel before. The deadline was two months away, in mid-March, and he only needed to

45

produce another 25,000 words to fulfill his contract.

But Bradbury was so daunted by the scope of the project that when the deadline passed, he hadn't written a single word. The publisher gave Bradbury a new deadline of April 15 — and he missed that deadline, too. The publisher gave Bradbury an extension to June 15 — and told Bradbury it was his last chance.

Paralyzed by fear all through May, unable to produce one page, a desperate Ray Bradbury finally went down into the basement of the UCLA library in early June. There, the university kept rows of coin-operated typewriters. Every half-hour, Bradbury fed a dime into the typewriter's meter. There was something about having to pay for his typewriter rental, dime after dime after dime, that forced him to finally get the work done.

Over a nine-day period, Bradbury wrote 25,000 words which he added to the 25,000 words of the original novella. He met his third and final deadline — and *Fahrenheit 451* was born. But first he had to overcome a writer's worst nightmare — the fear that he wouldn't be able to finish his book.

If you wrestle with this fear, you're no different than some of the greatest writers who ever lived, including Ray Bradbury and Ralph Ellison. You don't have to be defeated. Let me share with you some practical tools to help you overcome this fear so that you can begin your work, sustain it through the long writing process, and bring it to a successful and satisfying conclusion:

1. Recognize the voice of fear — and stop listening to it.

The voice of fear comes from your Inner Critic. Most people have a cruel Inner Critic living between their ears, whispering messages of defeat and condemnation throughout the day: "You're so stupid." "You can't do anything right."

"You don't deserve to be successful."

For some of us, the voice of the Inner Critic stops us dead in our tracks, paralyzing us with writer's block. "You call yourself a writer?" sneers the Critic. "You know you'll never finish that novel — and if you do, who would want to read it? Why waste your time?"

For others, the voice of the Inner Critic drives us to write obsessively and compulsively, producing page after page, hundreds and hundreds of pages. Yet we find no pleasure in the work, no sense of achievement or fulfillment, because the voice of the Inner Critic punishes us and tells us, "Everything you've written is garbage, you're an untalented hack. Work harder! Keep working until you produce something worth reading!"

The voice of the Inner Critic may sound to us like the voice of a hypercritical parent or a demanding teacher from our past. Listening to this voice of fear can ruin us as writers. In extreme cases, the voice of the Inner Critic can drive people into depression, eating disorders, and self-mutilation.

Writers who achieve success are often so used to hearing messages from the Inner Critic — "You'll never succeed, you don't deserve success" — that they are unable to enjoy success when it comes. They are afraid that the Inner Critic is right. They think, "It's only a matter of time before people find out what a fraud I am."

It helps to know that you're not alone, that even Nobel- and Pulitzer-winning authors have felt this way. Remember, as we saw in Chapter 1, that even John Steinbeck, while writing his Pulitzer-winning masterpiece *The Grapes of Wrath*, wrote in his journal, "I'm not a writer. I've been fooling myself." That was the voice of fear, the voice of Steinbeck's Inner Critic talking.

How do we silence the voice of fear that comes from the cruel and demanding Inner Critic? Here are some suggestions:

47

1. *Monitor your self-critical thoughts.* When you hear the voice of fear saying, "You won't finish, you don't deserve to be successful," write those thoughts down in a journal. Notice when those feelings occur to you. Can you detect any patterns? Do you have these feelings during certain seasons, or after conversations with certain people, or in connection with certain events? See if you can figure out what triggers these negative messages. If possible, avoid the situations that trigger those thoughts.

2. *Be objective about self-criticism.* When you hear the voice of fear saying, "You'll never finish that novel," pause and ask yourself where that thought comes from. Does it occur at times when you compare yourself with your favorite author or a fellow writer? Does it occur when you face a difficult challenge in your novel or a rough time in your "real life"? Is it a realistic thought — or is it ridiculously unrealistic?

3. *Turn condemnation into constructive criticism.* Take the Inner Critic's destructive, hurtful message and reframe it as a motivational maxim. You may hear the voice of fear say, "You're a loser. You never finish anything. You've tried to write two novels already, and you quit on them both." Simply invert that thought and turn it into a positive statement: "I've tried a couple of novels before, and I've learned a lot from both attempts. Now I'm going to take everything I've learned and apply it to a new novel — and this time I'm going to finish what I start." Transform the Inner Critic's put-downs into uplifting messages.

4. *Get involved in a writer's group or an event like National Novel Writing Month (NaNoWriMo).* Seek out any group of supportive fellow writers who encourage one another and cheer each other on. Every November, during National Novel Writing Month, thousands of writers accept the challenge of writing a complete first draft of a novel, at least 50,000 words, in thirty days. Many NaNoWriMo writers like

to connect with each other online, gather together in regional groups at libraries or bookstores, and compete against each other in online "word wars."

Suspense novelist James Scott Bell (*Try Dying* and *One More Lie*) writes that "NaNoWriMo is about community as much as it is about seclusion. It's about ritual as much as product. It's a month-long vibe and celebration of being a fiction writer."[2] The encouragement and support of fellow writers in the NaNoWriMo community may be just what you need to conquer your fear and supply the confidence you need to finish your novel. For information about National Novel Writing Month in November and Camp NaNoWriMo in April and July, visit the NaNoWriMo site at http://nanowrimo.org/.

5. *Replace self-criticism with self-affirmation.* The way we think about ourselves and talk to ourselves actually forms neural pathways in our brains. Negative, self-critical thinking forms pathways that set us up for pessimism, fear, self-doubt, and hopelessness. Self-affirming thinking forms pathways that reinforce optimism, courage, confidence, and motivation. The more positive our thinking, the greater our stamina and creative energy — and the more productive we are in every aspect of our lives, especially our writing.

Instead of thinking, "I'm afraid I can't finish my novel," tell yourself, "There's no 'quit' in me. I'm unstoppable. I *will* finish because I'm totally committed." And when the Inner Critic says, "You can't do this," just say, "Shut up! Go away! I'm writing."

2. Break big, intimidating goals into smaller steps.

We sometimes experience the fear of finishing as a result of the intimidating size and complexity of the project. If that's your fear, conquer it by breaking your big project down into non-intimidating, bite-size pieces. When you look at the size and scope of an entire novel, it can seem overwhelming and scary. But if you divide that novel into three acts, then divide each act into chapters, and each chapter into scenes, the project becomes manageable and do-able.

Don't think about the entire story arc, the plot twists, the subplots, or the sweeping themes of your story. Each day, think only about your word-count for that day. Maintain that same focus day after day, and in time you'll get your novel written from beginning to end.

Here's a guiding principle to follow whenever any sort of challenge intimidates or paralyzes you: *Reduce the size of your goal until you no longer fear it.* Think small. Turn big problems into little ones. Set nearer-term goals, pursue smaller ambitions, and keep moving forward, taking small steps instead of giant leaps. If the thought of writing a novel paralyzes you, set a goal of writing a chapter. If writing a chapter scares you, set a goal of writing a scene, a page, or a paragraph.

Fear triggers what physiologists call the "fight-or-flight response" — an acute stress response to a perceived threat. The frightened brain signals the nervous system, endocrine system, and vascular system, preparing the body to either fight the threat or flee from it — and sometimes the result is a lockup: our thinking shuts down and we freeze and cannot respond.

By reducing goals to a non-threatening size, we shut off the fight-or-flight response that comes from fear. We can function again. Whenever we overcome fear and successfully achieve our goals, we repattern our neural pathways, replacing fearful response patterns with confident response patterns. Over time, we gain the confidence to attempt increasingly bigger challenges without fear.

I recommend two excellent writing tools to help you break down long-term projects into achievable short-term objectives.

The first is an excellent book by James Scott Bell, *Plot & Structure*. The second is Randy Ingermanson's "Snowflake" method of structuring a novel, which you can find at AdvancedFictionWriting.com.

Ernest Hemingway once told an interviewer, "Once you are into the novel it is cowardly to worry about whether you can go on the next day. ... You *have* to go on. So there is no sense to worry. You have to learn that to write a novel. The hard part about a novel is to finish it."[3]

So write from your courage. Break big challenges into smaller steps. Keep writing forward until you've finished what you started.

3. Build your confidence by outlining your novel.

Novelists tend to fall into two camps, those who outline (or "pre-write") the plot of their novels, and those who simply write "by the seat of their pants" and figure out the plot as they go along. These two camps are often called "plotters" and "pantsers." I prefer to call them Outliners and Cliff-Jumpers (after Ray Bradbury's advice, "Jump off a cliff and build your wings on the way down").

Famous Outliners include thriller writers John Grisham, Robert Ludlum, and James Scott Bell, short story writer and novelist Katherine Anne Porter, historical fiction writer James Michener, fantasy writers J. R. R. Tolkien and Terry Brooks, and Randy Ingermanson, inventor of the "Snowflake" method of outlining. Famous Cliff-Jumpers include Ray Bradbury, Dean Koontz, Meg Cabot, Nora Roberts, Anne Rice, Patricia Cornwell, Anne McCaffrey, and Stephen King.

Suspense writer J. A. Jance, author of *Day of the Dead*, speaks for many Cliff-Jumpers when she explains why she rejects outlining: "I don't plan. I don't outline. I have hated outlines since sixth grade geography — and I can't do Roman numerals. I just like to see where the story goes."[4] Well, outlining a novel doesn't have to involve Roman numerals. You can plot your novel in any way that works for you.

Many Cliff-Jumpers reject outlining because they are impatient to jump into the story and see where it takes them. Others reject outlining because they believe that if they know in advance what the story is leading, they will unconsciously telegraph plot twists to the reader, and their story will become predictable. As Theodore Sturgeon once said, "If the writer has no idea what happens next, the reader certainly won't." There's a lot to be said for that view.

Yet there's also a lot to be said for the opposing view. Katherine Anne Porter (*Ship of Fools*) was a confirmed Outliner. She believed that until the ending is known, the writer does not have a story, because the story is all about the consequences of the character's actions. She told *The Paris Review*, "If I didn't know the ending of a story, I wouldn't begin. I always write my last lines, my last paragraph, my last page first, and then I go back and work towards it. I know where I'm going. I know what my goal is. And how I get there is God's grace."[5]

Outliners tend to be far less prone to writer's block and the fear of not finishing than Cliff-Jumpers are. The reason for this is obvious. If you know where you're going, if you have a roadmap for your novel, it's a lot less likely that you'll get lost, stuck, or blocked. If you are writing your way to a pre-selected destination, you have an excellent chance of getting there. The ending in your outline may not be the ending that appears in print — unforeseen possibilities may jump up and surprise you along the way. But at least you had a destination in mind to keep you from getting stuck.

The Cliff-Jumper, by contrast, leaps into the dark toward an unknown destination — and there's always a chance — a frightening possibility — of writing oneself into a corner.

Cliff-Jumpers often find themselves blocked by the fear that they might not come up with a plausible, satisfying ending.

If you are susceptible to the fear of not finishing, you might consider outlining your novel as a way of assuaging that fear. You don't need to pre-plan every scene in advance. Your outline can be as loose and open-ended as you like. It can take the form of a one-page synopsis, a twenty-page plot blueprint, a computer spreadsheet of key events, a Scrivener project file, or a stack of index cards. At certain stages in your outline, instead of laying out a specific chain of events, you may want to suggest multiple options or ask yourself questions to be answered as you write.

Your outline reassures you that you know where you're going and you'll be able to get there. By eliminating the fear of not finishing, you free yourself to be more confident and creative as you write. You never have to feel bound by the outline. You don't even have to look at it while you write the novel. Just knowing it's there, tucked away in a drawer or in a file on your hard drive, can give you peace of mind and the ability to write fearlessly.

If you choose to outline your novel, make sure that, during the outlining phase, you don't settle for obvious "plot twists" and easy solutions to story problems. As you brainstorm your plot, beware of ideas that come too easily and quickly. Keep daydreaming and imagining your story until you come up with a twist that surprises and delights you as a writer. Resist the temptation to rush through your outline just to get it over with. You are laying the foundation for your novel. Make sure it's a sturdy foundation.

When Cliff-Jumping novelists describe their creative process, they tend to sound like mystics. For example, Ray Bradbury described his creative process for *Fahrenheit 451* this way: "I just asked the characters to talk to me. ... I just listened to them."[6] But alongside the mystical explanation of

Bradbury's writing process, there is a practical explanation. In *The Bradbury Chronicles*, Sam Weller says that, in the early stages of writing *Fahrenheit 451*, Bradbury "made a quick outline for himself, a series of plot points he wanted to touch upon, then commenced writing madly."[7]

That's right. Ray Bradbury, the consummate Cliff-Jumper, *made an outline* when he approached a novel-length project. This is often the case with Cliff-Jumpers. They will tell you that they sit down in front of a blank computer screen, tabula rasa, and they invoke the Muse, writing whatever comes to mind. Rarely is this literally true, even though Cliff-Jumpers themselves may honestly remember it that way. The creative process is mysterious and difficult to describe in language other than metaphor. Over time, we writers begin to confuse our metaphorical descriptions of the creative process with literal fact.

Even if you're a Cliff-Jumper by temperament, consider Bradbury's approach to Fahrenheit 451: make a brief outline, a series of plot points to touch upon, just enough of a story skeleton to enable you to write fearlessly — then write madly.

4. Logically analyze your fear of not finishing.

Ask yourself: Is this fear logical and reality-based? Do you have rational grounds for feeling you might not finish your novel? Or is this fear nothing but irrational pessimism from your Inner Critic? If you decide your fear is not logical, stop listening to the voice of your Inner Critic. Once you are sure this is the voice of fear talking, shut it down.

Sometimes, however, the fear of not finishing is not irrational at all. It may, in fact, be an important signal from your unconscious mind, alerting you to potential obstacles and roadblocks up ahead. There may be a real basis for your fear, and you should not ignore what your unconscious mind is trying to tell you. Some examples:

The fear of not finishing may be a signal that the central idea of your novel is weak. Your characters, your theme, or your plot may not be substantial or interesting enough to support an entire novel. You may need to do more work to develop your idea to the point where it will sustain a novel from start to finish.

Or the fear of not finishing may be a signal that your story is unfocused. You are trying to do too much and say too much. Perhaps you have too many subplots in mind, and by the middle of the novel it could become too tangled and confusing to unravel. Perhaps you need to pare away some complications and focus on your main idea.

Or the fear of not finishing might be a signal that your protagonist is too bland, too passive, or too stereotypical. Your unconscious mind may be telling you that you need to re-imagine your hero or heroine, make this character more active, more bold, more unique and memorable, more fascinating.

Or the fear of not finishing may be a signal that there's not enough tension and conflict in your novel, or that the hero's stakes are not high enough to sustain the story.

Listen to your fear of not finishing. What is it saying to you? If it is merely saying, "You can't finish this, you'll never pull this off, you don't deserve success," then ignore it. But if the fear of finishing is saying, "There's a problem that needs to be fixed — a problem that may stop you dead in your tracks if you don't resolve it," then listen to your unconscious mind, find the source of the problem, fix it, and write on.

5. Focus on finishing.

Maybe you identify with this statement: "Some people say that writers are easily distracted, but I say — Ooh, shiny!" We writers love bright, shiny, new ideas. And distracting new ideas occur to us all the time. Some of our most interesting ideas occur right when we should be finishing our work-in-progress.

In my early writing career, it was not uncommon for me to shelve a project that was three-quarters finished in favor of some shiny new idea. "I'll just take a day or two and develop this new concept," I'd tell myself, "then I'll get right back to my novel." It rarely worked out as planned.

To be successful, we have to write quickly, sustain our forward motion trough the middle of the book, then finish strong. We have to ignore distractions — including attractive ideas for new projects. Great writing is a matter of momentum as well as imagination and emotion. Lose your momentum, lose your focus, and you'll have to struggle like mad to get back to where you were. In fact, you may never recapture the magic that was flowing so freely before you veered off-track.

Don't get distracted. Focus on finishing. Once you've completed your draft, you're free to explore all the shiny new ideas you want. Until then, keep writing forward. Write with blinders on. Be courageous. Go all the way.

Charles Bukowski's 1975 novel *Factotum* is the semi-autobiographical story of a boozing writer who drifts from one menial job to another in downtown L.A. while trying to write a novel. In the 2005 film adaptation, there's a scene in which Bukowski's alter ego, Hank Chinaski (played by Matt Dillon), talks about the writing life.

"If you're going to try," he says, "go all the way." After all, he reasons, why start if you don't go all the way? Then Chinaski lists the things it might cost you to go all the way as a writer. It might cost you your girlfriend or wife, your job, your sanity. Going all the way could mean going hungry, freezing on a park bench, and enduring mockery and isolation. It will almost certainly mean rejection and trying to overcome the worst possible odds.

But when you win, says Chinaski, it's better than anything else imaginable — for the writer who reaches that pinnacle is in the realm of the gods where the nights flame with fire. He concludes, "It's the only good fight there is."[8]

Chinaski's right. If you're going to write, shed your fear — and *finish*.

If you're going to try, go all the way.

---

1. Norman Podhoretz, *The Norman Podhoretz Reader: A Selection of His Writings From the 1950s Through the 1990s* (New York: Free Press, 2004), 365.

2. James Scott Bell, "How to Write a Novel in a Month," The Kill Zone, October 14, 2012, killzoneauthors.blogspot.com/2012/10/how-to-write-novel-in-month.html.

3. Ernest Hemingway, *By-Line Ernest Hemingway: Selected Articles and Dispatches of Four Decades* (New York: Scribner, 2002), Kindle edition.

4. Michael Grady, "Tucson Suspense Writer J.A. Jance Got Started in Her Own Back Yard," *East Valley Tribune* (Phoenix-Mesa-Tempe), August 3, 2004, http://www.eastvalleytribune.com/article_0ef700f0-51fa-5ef9-9eda-bdaf5de775ef.html?mode=print.

5. Barbara Thompson Davis, "Katherine Anne Porter, The Art of Fiction No. 29," *The Paris Review*, Winter-Spring 1963, http://www.theparisreview.org/interviews/4569/the-art-of-fiction-no-29-katherine-anne-porter.

6. Sam Weller, *Listen to the Echoes: The Ray Bradbury Interviews* (Brooklyn: Melville House, 2010), 123.

7. Sam Weller, *The Bradbury Chronicles* (New York: Morrow, 2005), 205.

8. Matt Dillon as Henry Chinaski in the motion picture *Factotum* (2005), written by Bent Hamer and Jim Stark, YouTube video, "If You Are Going To Try It, Go All The Way — Factotum," posted by ToGroundControl, transcribed by Jim Denney, https://www.youtube.com/watch?v=DX6JdynMW-M.

Fear No. 4
"I Fear the Risks of the Writer's Life"

"Here is the world.
Beautiful and terrible things will happen.
Don't be afraid."
Frederick Buechner

Piers Anthony is an English-American science fiction writer who has enjoyed a long-running career. To date, he has had roughly a hundred fifty novels published and he currently writes two or three novels per year. Many of his books have been *New York Times* bestsellers. But success didn't come easily for Piers Anthony.

In 1962, when Piers was twenty-eight, his wife agreed to work and support them while he attempted to build a full-time writing career. She set only one condition: If Piers didn't sell anything after one year of writing, he would quit writing and take a non-writing job. During his first year as a writer, he sold two short stories, earning a grand total of $160.

Though he had technically met his wife's one condition by selling those two stories, he was a long way from earning a living as a writer. So he took a position as an English teacher.

58

After three years of teaching, he lost his job due to budget cutbacks. Realizing that even a non-writing job offered no real security, he decided to try writing again. He concluded that it had been a mistake to try to earn a living by writing stories. The money, he realized, was in novels.

So he went to work and crafted an intricately structured futuristic novel, a tale of forbidden love and grim conditions in a subterranean prison on a distant planet. He sold his debut novel, entitled *Chthon*, to Ballantine (after three other houses rejected it). Ballantine published the book in 1967, to instant acclaim and brisk sales. *Chthon* was nominated for both the Hugo and Nebula awards.

A few years ago, I interviewed Piers Anthony and asked him what preparations he made for entering a full-time writing career. "Preparations?" he said. "I didn't make any. My entry into full-time writing was set up by the worst day of my life, when I lost my job, my wife lost our third baby stillborn, and a doctor told me my depression was all in my head and that it would pass when I saw that my problems weren't real. The idiot! But without a job and without a child, I was free to gamble on trying to become a writer while my wife worked to support us. Out of those ashes came my career — in time."

Piers Anthony wrote his breakthrough novel when he was desperate, out of work, and had his back against the wall. He succeeded because he pursued his goals with a grand strategy of writing in a profitable format — the novel. After the publication of *Chthon*, his prolific writing career was off and running.

The writer's life is an inherently risky proposition. When you write, you take personal risks, commercial risks, and artistic risks. It's almost impossible to achieve distinction as an author if you are risk-averse. As Kurt Vonnegut once observed, "Talent is extremely common. What is rare is the willingness to endure the life of a writer."

Are you willing to endure the risks of the writing life? "It takes a lot of energy and a lot of neurosis to write a novel," said Laurence Durrell (author of *The Alexandria Quartet*). "If you were really sensible, you'd go do something else." So what do you want to be? Do you want to be sensible? Or do you want to be a writer?

And if you want to write, what holds you back? Is it fear of the risks of the writer's life?

Some crucial questions you must ask yourself

Playwright A. R. Gurney, author of *The Cocktail Hour* and *Sweet Sue*, recalls the years when he taught literature at MIT while writing plays on the side. A novelist friend told him, "You gotta start calling yourself a writer, you gotta start thinking of yourself as a writer. You're never gonna get anywhere if you don't take yourself seriously."

Gurney reflects, "I found it very hard ... to call myself a writer. I called myself a teacher. ... It was very hard for me to accept the public mantle of being a playwright." Once Gurney was able to confidently call himself a writer and embrace the risky life of a writer, his self-image was transformed — and his writing career shifted into high gear.[1]

Writing is all about risk and fear. If the prospect of being a writer has never scared you, then you have never considered all the risks that writing entails.

Novelist Dani Shapiro once described the three great risks of the writer's life: "The writer's apprenticeship — or perhaps, the writer's lot — is this miserable trifecta: uncertainty, rejection, disappointment. ... Every single piece of writing I have ever completed — whether a novel, a memoir, an essay, short story, or review — has begun as a wrestling match between hopelessness and something else. ... Call it stubbornness, stamina, a take-no-prisoners determination, but a writer at work reminds me of nothing so much as a terrier with a bone."[2]

To be a writer is to battle fear and doubt, and to risk uncertainty, rejection, and disappointment. So *you* have to be that terrier. You have to chomp down on that bone and refuse to let go.

If you would achieve your dreams, you must risk, you must endure, and you must never give up. Dare to believe that your purpose in life is to write — then dare to write that first sentence. Persevere, keep faith with your dreams, and dare to complete what you started. Stop endlessly revising your manuscript — declare it finished and share it with your critique group. Then fearlessly subject your work to the brutal analysis of agents and editors — and the reading public.

Above all, dare to say to yourself and others, "I *am* a writer."

I have been a full-time self-employed writer since 1989. It's been a risky existence. Sometimes the risks have paid off, sometimes not. But I'm still here, still writing every day.

I've met a few writers who have no desire to write full-time. They like working at a regular job, then coming home and writing evenings and weekends. Some tell me they need the security of a regular paycheck. Others tell me they don't know if they could remain disciplined if they had all day to write — limited writing time, they say, *forces* them to make the most of the time they have. There's a lot to be said for that choice.

Most of the writers I've met aspire to write full-time, as I do. There's a lot to be said for that choice as well. But before you take the step of quitting your day job, you need to weigh the risks and count the costs. Here are some questions to ask yourself:

1. *Do I have a high tolerance for risk, uncertainty, and stress?* If the answer is no, don't take the plunge into full-time

writing. Hold on to your day job and keep writing part-time. "You have to have a pretty high threshold for financial insecurity," says novelist Lawrence Block. "If a regular paycheck is emotionally essential to you, perhaps you'd be well advised to stay with a regular job."[3]

Even if you do have a high tolerance for risk, it's best to budget ruthlessly and live frugally, at least until you get a seven-figure check from your first bestseller. Build up your savings and investments. Pay off any high-interest debt, such as credit cards and finance company debt (don't even consider full-time writing if you are buried in debt). Be disciplined and mature when it comes to spending and finances.

2. *Do I have substantial savings or income sources to carry me through the lean times?* Your financial safety net could come in a number of different forms: savings and investments; an early retirement incentive from your present employer; a mortgage, second mortgage, or reverse mortgage on your home; a working spouse who will lovingly support your dream; or a gift from a generous benefactor.

Some writers scrimp and save their day job earnings for several years in order to squirrel away twelve to twenty-four months of living expenses — then they plunge into full-time writing for a year or two. Make sure you have an adequate safety net (including health care coverage) before you take the leap into full-time writing.

3. *Do I write at least an hour every day?* A good way to see if you have the discipline to be a full-time writer is to "test-drive" your writing career while you are still employed. Write daily — mornings, evenings, and weekends — and see if you have the discipline and drive to be a full-time writer.

Hugo- and Nebula-winning science fiction writer Robert J. Sawyer once told me, "Real writers buy the time, if they can't get it any other way. I know a high-school teacher in Toronto who takes every fifth year off from teaching without pay in order to write. Writers make sacrifices for their art."

4. *Have I built a reputation for delivering excellent work on deadline?* By 1989, I had six published books to my credit (written while I was working at a day job), and I had several book editors and a magazine editor who would call me and offer me assignments. I had built a reputation for meeting deadlines, and turning in good work. When you're known for your professionalism and competence, you become sought-after by editors. My good relationships with editors gave me the confidence I needed to launch out on my own.

Missing deadlines is a sure-fire way to tarnish your reputation as a writer. If you need an extra week or two, call your editor and ask for an extension. The more responsible and dependable you are, the more work you'll get.

5. *Does my "significant other" support my writing goals?* The support of your spouse or partner is crucial. He or she is going to be along for this rollercoaster ride, and will share in the risks. Emotional support is a major factor in a writer's success — or failure. Your partner may have to work harder and longer to provide financial support and benefits while you establish your career. In *On Writing*, Stephen King offers this grateful tribute to his wife Tabitha:

My wife made a crucial difference. ... If she had suggested that the time I spent writing stories on the front porch of our rented house on Pond Street or in the laundry room of our rented trailer on Klatt Road in Hermon was wasted time, I think a lot of the heart would have gone out of me. Tabby never voiced a single doubt, however. Her support was a constant, one of the few good things I could take as a given. And whenever I see a first novel dedicated to a wife (or a husband), I smile and think, *There's someone who knows*. Writing is a lonely job. Having someone who believes in you makes a lot of difference.[4]

A writer with a spouse and a family, does not accept all the risks of the writer's life alone. The entire household is along for the ride — and every family member shares the risk. Make sure you have the support of everyone involved.

6. *Do I have the temperament to handle the frustrations of the writer's life?* One of those frustrations is the need to be courteous to abrasive people.

Some years ago, I answered the phone and heard the familiar voice of an editor I had worked with on a number of books. She was usually quite friendly. Not this time. "Jim," she said, "I know how you spoke to my assistant, and if that ever happens again, you'll never get another assignment from me."

I was baffled. I had a cordial working relationship with the assistant, and we had never exchanged a single harsh word. "I don't know what you're talking about," I said. "I haven't—"

"I don't want excuses," the editor said. "I don't even want an apology. I just want you to know it had better not happen again." Then, before I could say another word, she changed the subject. We talked about other matters, but it was hard to concentrate after feeling the rough side of my editor's tongue.

After the call, I tried to go back to my writing, but the mystery of the editor's reprimand nagged at me. So I finally called the editor's assistant and said, "I called to apologize."

"Apologize? What for?"

"I'm not sure. But your boss said I was rude to you on the phone. I don't remember doing that, but if I said anything that offended you, I want you to know I didn't mean it and I'm sorry."

"Honest, Jim, I have no idea what this is about. You've always been easy to work with. I've never complained to my boss about you. I don't know what this is about. Maybe I'd better ask her — "

"No," I said, "I think it would be best to let it go. As long as you're not offended, it's okay with me to drop it."

So we dropped it. And to this day, I don't know what that was all about. But I think I handled it the right way. If I had insisted on defending myself and proving my innocence, I might have ruined my relationship with that editor. As it was, the matter blew over, and I went on to do many more books with the editor and her assistant.

Another challenge of the working writer's life is the need to accept rejection and tough criticism of your work. And you must accept it *graciously.*

Once, early in my career, I sent a completed manuscript to an editor, right on deadline. I was proud of that book and felt I had done a good job. Also, money was tight and I needed the back end of the advance. I was hoping the editor would send me a check by return mail. No such luck.

The editor called and said, "We need to talk — face-to-face. I'm flying out and we're going to spend a day talking about how to fix this book." My heart sank. I knew there'd be no check until I had "fixed" the book to his satisfaction.

A few days later, we had a draining, all-day session. The editor diagrammed the book on a whiteboard so that I could see the structure and content — what the book was, and what it needed to be. He showed me that two chapters didn't fit the overall theme of the book — he wanted me to cut those, just trash 'em. And I needed to write two *new* chapters to replace the ones I trashed. Two other chapters needed heavy rewriting. The editor wanted the revised manuscript in six weeks.

I was discouraged, to say the least. But I had to admit it: He was right — the book needed every one of those changes. So I went home and made all the changes as the editor had requested — and I completed the work in two weeks, not six. And it was clearly a better book.

To be a professional writer, you have to accept criticism. You must understand that criticism of the work is not criticism of *you*. Every writer gets edited. It's part of the job.

If the risks of the writer's life scare you — good. They should. The risks entailed in writing should give you serious pause. But if you are willing to accept those risks, then I wish you well on your writing journey — and I have some hard-won advice to share with you. These are the lessons I learned the hard way in my own journey as a writer:

1. Stay focused and calm under pressure.

Good writing takes place in a state of relaxation and intense focus. In order to draw upon the resources of your creative Muse, your unconscious mind, you need to be calm and centered, yet so focused and concentrated that you block out all distractions. Pressure and conflict can stop the flow of your writing. Financial worries, unpaid bills, collection calls, arguments with family members, and battles with editors are corrosive to the creative process.

Let's face it: You can't always eliminate pressures and distractions from your life. But you can learn to block them out of your consciousness while you're working and creating. Playwright Tennessee Williams once told interviewer Dotson Rader, "I try to work every day, because you have no refuge but writing. When you're going through a period of unhappiness, a broken love affair, the death of someone you love, or some other disorder in your life, then you have no refuge but writing."[5]

Don't let worries and problems keep you from work. If you're going through tough times, dive even deeper into your writing. Pour all your pain into your stories. Take refuge in your writing. If your soul feels like screaming, let it scream through your writing.

I vividly recall the days following the 9/11 terror attacks. It was an emotionally oppressive time. Many of my writer friends simply stopped writing for days and even weeks following the attacks. I was facing a tight deadline on a multi-book fiction project, a series of science fiction adventures for young readers. I couldn't afford to stop writing.

So I took the emotions of that terrible time and I poured those emotions into the books I was writing. A lot of dark and disturbing scenes and plot twists came to mind, and I wrote them all down. I knew I couldn't turn in the book that way — I was writing for kids, after all — but I wrote my way through the darkness. It was cathartic. Writing became a refuge from the sadness and horror on my TV screen.

After I finished the first draft, I did a rewrite and removed the material that was too disturbing. But I kept an appropriate amount of that dark material, because it enriched the tale and gave it more emotional depth.

Never use tough times as an excuse to stop writing. Use your pain to give your writing more emotional texture and realism. Don't panic when life gets hard. Don't yield to fear. Strike back by writing through the fear.

2. Approach writing as a profession.

Writing is art — but writing is also an act of commerce. It's a serious business, so approach it in a businesslike way. The art of writing has to do with imagination, creativity, and craft. The business of writing involves scheduling projects, dealing with editors, budgeting time, and managing cash flow. Even if an attorney or agent negotiates your contracts, you need to understand everything that's in those contracts.

Professional writers rely on professional advice. Have your accountant set up your bookkeeping system and alert you to the tax advantages available to you. Expert financial advice doesn't cost — it pays.

Most important of all, maintain order and structure in your business life. It will help you stay centered and focused in your writing life. By managing your writing as a business, you put more of your writing life under your control. The more competently you manage the business side of your life — your cash flow, your expenses, your deadlines, your tax liability — the less anxiety and fear you will experience. Fear is a distraction, so eliminate as much business-related fear as you can.

[**Author's Note:** For a thorough discussion of the risks and rewards of writing for a living, see my book *Quit Your Day Job!: How to Sleep Late, Do What You Enjoy, and Make a Ton of Money as a Writer.* —J.D.]

3. Avoid self-pity.

Never waste time feeling sorry for yourself, feeling jealous of other writers, or making comparisons to other writers. Don't compare your sales, Amazon.com ranking, or reviews to anyone else's. As a writer, you have only one focus: The work.

It's great to write a bestseller. But great writers focus on the writing, the purity of the work, not the sales figures. It takes time, hard work, and persistence to build a writing career and achieve your goals. That's as it should be. Writing is *supposed* to be hard. If it was easy to write a book, everybody would do it.

On some days, you'll be tempted to envy other writers. You'll even be tempted to envy your non-writing friends, because of their regular paychecks and secure jobs. Beware of the trap of comparing yourself to others.

You are a writer. You're doing what you love. How many of your friends can say that? Most of your friends, if they won the lottery today, would instantly quit their jobs. If you won the lottery, would you quit writing? Of course not. A sudden windfall would merely give you more freedom to write!

Your friends may have a "career," but you have something better than a career. You have a calling. You have a purpose in life. You are a writer.

Self-pity, jealousy, and comparisons to others stir up negative emotions. One negative emotion easily brings up another. Once you have talked yourself into self-pity or bitterness, you've put yourself right on the brink of fear.

Don't go there. Stay positive. Practice gratitude for the good things in your life, including the fact that you're a writer. You don't have time for self-pity or fear. Keep your eyes on your dreams and goals. Stay strong, stay fearless.

4. Cultivate friendships, relationships, and contacts.

If you want to be successful, talent and hard work are not enough. You need to take control of your writing career. That means you need to get to know as many different people in the book business as you can — editors, agents, fellow writers, and influential people in all walks of life. You never know where your next sale or winning book idea may come from. Here's an example from the world of acting that demonstrates the importance of cultivating friendships of all times, at all levels:

Shortly before the start of World War II, Kirk Douglas was one of hundreds of struggling, obscure actors competing for parts on the Broadway stage. He lived in a cramped little room in Greenwich Village, waited tables at Schrafft's, auditioned for countless parts, but got nowhere in his career. Still, Douglas made many friends among the aspiring actors and actresses he hung out with. One of his friends was a young ingenue named Betty Joan Perske.

After the attack on Pearl Harbor, Kirk Douglas enlisted in the Navy and saw action in the Pacific. After the war, he came home and discovered that Betty Joan Perske was now a box-office sensation in a major picture, starring with Humphrey Bogart. The film was *To Have and Have Not*, and Betty Joan Perske was now known as Lauren Bacall.

Now that Lauren Bacall was a big star, she could put Kirk Douglas in touch with some of Hollywood's most powerful people. She introduced him to producer Hal Wallis, who cast him in *The Strange Love of Martha Ivers*. And Kirk Douglas was on his way to stardom.

"Your own luck depends on other people's luck," the actor later recalled. "Oh, sure, I guess I had some kind of talent. But if it hadn't been for … [Lauren Bacall], where would the talent have gone?"[6]

We tend to think that only powerful, influential people are in a position to help us. We need to realize that anyone, even an unknown fellow writer, could one day become influential in the publishing world, and a big influence in our own careers.

Of the hundred-plus books I have published, only a handful have been sold to editors who didn't personally know me. The vast majority were sold through relationships. So I encourage you to get to know people in the writing world. Get to know people in traditional publishing and indie publishing. Attend writers conferences and workshops, and talk to as many people as you can. Sign up for one-on-one sessions to pitch your novels to editors and agents. Get acquainted with fellow writers at all levels, including aspiring writers.

Join or start a writers' support group. In a writers' group, members share their goals and hold each other accountable. A writers' group can also be a critique group, in which members share their writings with each other for constructive feedback. Writers' groups are a powerful tool for mutual encouragement and growth.

Trust is essential to such groups, so there are certain covenants or rules that members should agree to. Commit to being honest with each other — not "brutally" honest, but truthful and candid in a constructive way. Commit to holding each other accountable for progress toward your writing goals. Your writer's group can help you deal with the struggles, self-doubt, and fears that are a part of the writer's life.

Be willing to help fellow writers, asking nothing in return. Share contacts, resources, and information. You'll be amazed at how often the good you do comes back to you. The more connections you make, the "luckier" you'll be.

5. Become a public speaker.

E. B. "Andy" White was the author of such works as *Charlotte's Web* and *Stuart Little*. He became a writer in an era when public appearances were not a major part of the writer's life. Writers rarely needed to venture out in public — which was just fine with Andy White.

He was plagued by fears throughout his life, and one of the worst was his fear of public speaking. He was terrified to be anywhere near a crowd. White's stepson, Roger Angell, recalled, "For years, he had passed up family weddings and graduations, town meetings, dedications and book awards, cocktail bashes and boat gams and garden parties."

As White's literary reputation grew, universities wanted to confer honorary degrees on him — which meant he had to appear in public, receive a diploma, and say a few words. "Despite prearranged infusions of sherry or Scotch," Angell recalled, "he found the ceremonials excruciating." Yet White felt obligated to attend.

When Dartmouth conferred an honorary doctorate on E. B. White in 1948, he was on the platform in his cap and gown, waiting in terror for his name to be called. He later described his emotions in a letter: "The old emptiness and dizziness and vapors seized hold of me. ... Nobody who has never had my peculiar kind of disability can understand the sheer hell of such moments."

When he was introduced, he stood to receive the hood that symbolized his doctorate — but as the hood was placed over his head, a breeze blew the hood up, covering his face. In White's own words, he became a "fully masked Doctor of Letters, a headless poet."

After that embarrassing incident, E. B. White refused to speak or appear in public. He declined an invitation in 1963 to go to the White House and receive the Presidential Medal of Freedom from Lyndon Johnson. He even missed the graveside funeral service for his wife in 1977. Roger Angell recalled, "None of us in the family expected otherwise or held this against him. And when his own memorial came, eight years later, I took the chance to remark, 'If Andy White could be with us today, he would not be with us today."[7]

Another great writer who suffered from the fear of public speaking was the author of the Declaration of Independence and the third President of the United States, Thomas Jefferson. Throughout his two-term presidency, he is known to have delivered only two speeches — his two inaugural addresses. And they scarcely deserve to be called "speeches." He wrote out his text, then read it in front of the crowd, speaking so softly that hardly anyone could hear what he said.

In today's world, authors must also be speakers. You have to get up before audiences to tell people about your book. Public speaking is one of the risks of a writer's life.

Does the thought of speaking to audiences frighten you? Let me suggest some actions you can take to overcome your fear of public speaking.

First, get practice speaking before small groups. Offer to lecture and sign books at your local library or bookstore. I've given quite a few library and bookstore talks over the years, and I guarantee, the audiences *will* be small. If crowds frighten you, this is the place to start.

Practice public speaking in other non-threatening settings. Attend local lectures, and stand up to ask the speaker a question. Offer to give readings or announcements at your local house of worship or community club. Practice talking briefly in front of groups, just to get comfortable with speaking. Call in to radio talk shows and give the radio audience a piece of your mind.

As you gain confidence, accept bigger and bigger challenges. If someone asks you to speak at an event, accept the invitation. Don't turn down opportunities for growth and improvement. Seek out opportunities. Join a Toastmasters club (there are more than 14,000 Toastmasters clubs worldwide; see http://www.toastmasters.org/). Or take a public speaking course through your local community college or an executive training company such as Decker Communications (founded by my longtime friend and writing partner Bert Decker; see http://decker.com/).

Another friend and writing partner, Pat Williams, is the founder of the Orlando Magic and a noted author and speaker. He encourages people to speak from the heart, not from note cards. He's not suggesting we memorize a speech then recite it word for word. Instead, we need to have a *conversation* with the audience.

Here's Pat's advice: "Organize your message and get the structure of your talk fixed in your mind. Know exactly where your stories and key points go in the talk. Practice it repeatedly. Follow your mental outline of your talk, but form your words and sentences as you go. Speak from your heart. Talk to your audience as if you were having a one-on-one conversation. It will be the same essential message every time you deliver it, but it will be a different speech, framed in different words — and it will sound fresh, spontaneous, and natural every time you deliver it.

"With practice, you'll gain the confidence to talk to any audience of any size, without notes and without fear. You'll speak confidently and wow your audience. You'll even be able to walk around naturally, making eye contact with your listeners. When you speak without notes, you command attention. Your listeners will sit up straight, not wanting to miss a word."

Ray Bradbury exemplified this conversational approach to public speaking. Early in his career, Bradbury was invited to give a talk at the University of Southern California. About a hundred people were present. After Bradbury was introduced, he went to the lectern and began reading from his carefully prepared notes. After a few minutes, he looked up and saw that every face in the audience seemed half-asleep.

"Attention!" Bradbury shouted. "Watch this!"

A hundred people sat up straight, eyes popped wide.

Bradbury threw his notes down and stomped on them.

"Now, to continue," he said — and he proceeded to speak for the rest of the hour without notes. He had a *conversation* with his listeners, and they were spellbound. Bradbury never spoke from notes again.[8]

If you want to overcome your fear of public speaking, stop reading speeches from notes. Have a conversation with your audience.

6. Never give up on your dream of being a writer.

Lionel Shriver is an American-born British author. Her first novel, *The Female of the Species*, was published in 1986. During the next two decades, she produced five more novels — all commercial flops. She decided her next book, *We Need to Talk About Kevin*, was her make-or-break book. If it failed,

Shriver was resigned to going back to newspaper writing.

We Need to Talk About Kevin is a thriller about a student who plans to commit mass murder at his high school. "Writing that novel was a slog," she told an interviewer. "I have more determination than the average bear, but anyone's internal resources are finite. Having long resorted to journalism to make ends meet, I was already mentally preparing for a future as a full-time hack. But I finished my first draft because I wouldn't be accused of not having tried."[9]

Forcing herself to finish paid off. *We Need to Talk About Kevin* was published in 2004 and it touched a nerve with the reading public. Not only was the book a huge commercial and critical success, but it also garnered the 2005 Orange Prize (also known as the Baileys Women's Prize for Fiction).

Why did *Kevin* succeed when her previous novels failed? Interviewed by *The Irish Times*, Shriver said, "Did something happen around the time I wrote *Kevin*? Did I have some revelation or transforming event? The truth is that *Kevin* is of a piece with my other work. There's nothing special about *Kevin*. The other books are good too. It just tripped over an issue that was ripe for exploration and by some miracle found its audience."[10]

The moral of the story: Never give up on your writing dreams. Don't let rejection, discouragement, commercial failure, worry, or fear keep you from the pursuit of your goals.

As Shriver said, "I paid my dues. Not to put too fine a point on it, I was in commercial terms a flat-out failure as a novelist for nearly twenty years."[11] *We Need to Talk About Kevin* would never have seen print, much less found its vast audience, if Lionel Shriver hadn't slogged through almost twenty years of discouragement. She made up her mind to finish — and because she did, she captured the elusive dream of success.

Stay focused. Stay positive. Never surrender to self-doubt or self-pity. Write fearlessly, and keep fighting for your dreams.

---

1. Frederic Hunter, "Playwright A. R. Gurney Interview," *Christian Science Monitor*, January 23, 1989, http://www.csmonitor.com/1989/0123/ugurne.html.

2. Dani Shapiro, "A Writing Career Becomes Harder to Scale," *Los Angeles Times*, February 7, 2010, http://articles.latimes.com/2010/feb/07/entertainment/la-ca-endurability7-2010feb07.

3. Lawrence Block, *Telling Lies for Fun and Profit* (New York: Morrow, 1981), 78.

4. Stephen King, *On Writing: A Memoir of the Craft* (10th Anniversary Edition: New York: Pocket Books, 2000), 64-65.

5. Dotson Rader, "Tennessee Williams, The Art of Theater No. 5," *The Paris Review*, Fall 1981, http://www.theparisreview.org/interviews/3209/the-art-of-theater-no-5-tennessee-williams.

6. Max Gunther, *The Luck Factor* (New York: Macmillan, 1977), 25.

7. Roger Angell, *Let Me Finish* (New York: Houghton Mifflin Harcourt, 2006), 118-119.

8. Sam Weller, *Listen to the Echoes: The Ray Bradbury Interviews* (Brooklyn: Melville House, 2010), 84.

9. Laurie Pawlik-Kierlen, "How to Increase Writing Confidence — Grow the Skin of a Rhino," TheAdventurousWriter.com, July 6, 2011, http://theadventurouswriter.com/blogwriting/how-to-increase-writing-confidence-grow-the-skin-of-a-rhino/.

10. Those DeWolfes, "Best Sellers List: Lionel Shriver," ThoseDeWolfes.com, http://www.thosedewolfes.com/bestsellers/?au=Lionel+Shriver.

11. Laurie Pawlik-Kienlen, "Courage to Write — Tips From an Anxious Bestselling Author," TheAdventurousWriter.com, November 19, 2010, http://theadventurouswriter.com/blogwriting/finding-courage-to-write-ways-to-cope-with-writing-fears/.

Fear No. 5
"I'm Afraid to Reveal Who I Am"

———

"I am not a character
in this novel; I am the novel."
Philip K. Dick

———

Joan Didion is a highly regarded writer who explores themes of anxiety and fragmentation in relationships. She has written novels (*A Book of Common Prayer*), nonfiction books (*Slouching Towards Bethlehem*), screenplays (*The Panic in Needle Park*), and stage plays (*The Year of Magical Thinking*, examining her grief following the death of her husband of forty years). She spent most of her youth growing up in Sacramento, California, and graduated from the University of California at Berkeley in the 1950s.

As she neared graduation at Berkeley, Didion discovered that she lacked a required course for her major, a class on the works of English poet John Milton. So, every Friday during the summer of 1956, she took the train or the Greyhound bus to Berkeley for a course on Milton's *Paradise Lost*.

During those trips, she took note of the sinister-looking oil refineries around Carquinez Straits, the rhythm and sounds of the train, and even "the exact rancidity of the butter" in the dining car. At that time, she lacked the confidence to envision a career as a writer. She didn't know who she was or what she might become. Didion recalls:

> During those years I was traveling on what I knew to be a very shaky passport, forged papers: I knew that I was no legitimate resident in any world of ideas. I knew I couldn't think. All I knew then was what I couldn't do. All I knew then was what I wasn't, and it took me some years to discover what I was.
> Which was a writer.
> By which I mean not a "good" writer or a "bad" writer but simply a writer, a person whose most absorbed and passionate hours are spent arranging words on pieces of paper. Had my credentials been in order I would never have become a writer. Had I been blessed with even limited access to my own mind there would have been no reason to write. I write entirely to find out what I'm thinking, what I'm looking at, what I see and what it means. What I want and what I fear.[1]

Many writers write for the purpose of self-discovery. The celebrated English novelist Dodie Smith (*I Capture the Castle* and *The Hundred and One Dalmatians*) explained her motive for writing: "Perhaps if I make myself write I shall find out what is wrong with me."

Novelist and essayist James Baldwin (*Go Tell It on the Mountain*) observed that, in the creative process, the writer not only discovers who he or she is, but is forever changed by that discovery: "You go into a book and you're in the dark, really. You go in with a certain fear and trembling. You know one thing. You know you will not be the same person when this voyage is over. But you don't know what's going to happen to you between getting on the boat and stepping off. And you have to trust that."[2]

Once a writer discovers the Self through the act of writing, a terrifying realization occurs: The writer *must disclose* on the printed page what he or she has discovered. The writer must reveal the Self.

As Ursula Le Guin observed, "About nineteen writers out of twenty are introverts." The vicious irony of the writer's life is that most writers are intensely private people — yet their calling is to look within, dredge up their darkest secrets, and scrawl them on the page for the entire world to see.

The worst nightmare for many writers is self-disclosure. When you write a book or story, you often expose more of the Self than you intend or realize. You may think you have done an excellent job of hiding behind your fictional characters — but your readers may find you as transparent as glass. The more honest you are, the more of yourself you reveal — your joy and pain, your hopes and fears, the things that touch you, the things that wound you, the things that outrage you. The truth of who you are will bleed through the ink stains on the page. If you try to hide, you will be found out.

So it's only natural for writers to wonder, "What if I reveal too much? And what if my readers don't like what they see?" This fear is common to all writers who are serious about their craft.

Dip up the fire

In *A Year of Writing Dangerously*, writing teacher Barbara Abercrombie writes that she once asked a group of student writers if writing felt "dangerous" to them. The students all agreed that it did. When she asked why, one student replied, "Writing is dangerous because you might get caught."

Abercrombie concludes: "*Caught, found out, exposed.* The stuff of nightmares ... our secrets exposed, our inner life and imagination up for inspection."[3] She goes on to quote writer Ralph Keyes, who said, "Anxiety is not only an inevitable part of the writing process but a necessary part. *If you're not scared, you're not writing.*"[4]

Don't fear the truth within you. Don't fear the painful memories that are pulled up from your unconscious mind as you write. When you unlock your inner truth, your writing comes alive with honesty and originality. You are finally giving your readers what they want, need, and deserve. You are giving them the gift of *yourself.*

Whenever you give of yourself, you put yourself at risk. This is especially true when you break open the shell of your soul and reveal what is inside. In an interview, novelist E. L. Doctorow put it this way: "Writers are not just people who sit down and write. They hazard themselves. Every time you compose a book, your composition of yourself is at stake. ... Writing is a lifelong act of self-displacement."[5]

Not every writer fears self-revelation. Some relish it. One of the most fearless and extroverted writers I know, Harlan Ellison, explains his approach to writing this way:

> I talk about the things people have always talked about in stories: pain, hate, truth, courage, destiny, friendship, responsibility, growing old, growing up, falling in love, all of these things. What I try to write about are the darkest things in the soul, the mortal dreads. I try to go into those places in me that contain the cauldrous. I want to dip up the fire, and I want to put it on paper. The closer I get to the burning core of my being, the things which are most painful to me, the better is my work.

80

It is a love/hate relationship I have with the human race. I am an elitist, and I feel that my responsibility is to drag the human race along with me — that I will never pander to, or speak down to, or play the safe game. Because my immortal soul will be lost.[6]

To write fearlessly, heed Harlan's example. Embrace the burning truth within you, then express it boldly and honestly through your writing.

Honest writing can be painful, but it's a healing, surgical pain. Pediatric surgeon and author Bernie Siegel began writing to heal his own pain of dealing with suffering, dying children every day. "Scalpels and words are instruments which can cure or kill," he once observed. "If you cannot bring forth your feelings, they will destroy you."[7] And Les Cuadra, author of *Crystal Heroes*, put it this way: "The truth is like a scalpel that cuts, and causes a bleeding that usually heals."

Irwin Shaw talked about the pain of writing in an interview with *The Paris Review*, "Writing is like a contact sport, like football. Why do kids play football? They can get hurt on any play, can't they? Yet they can't wait until Saturday comes around so they can play ... and get smashed around. Writing is like that. You can get hurt, but you enjoy it."[8]

By recognizing your fear of revealing yourself and by willing yourself to face your pain, you can disarm your fears. You can say to yourself, "I now know why I've been timid and fearful. I know why I've resisted writing. I've been afraid to reveal myself. Yet I became a writer so that I could speak my truth. From now on, I'll push past my resistance and fear."

You can't be the writer you were meant to be as long as you are held back by the fear of self-revelation. You must be willing to hazard yourself, to dip up the fire from the burning core of your being, and to fearlessly put it all on the page.

Here are some ways you can summon the courage to write your own original truth:

1. Don't hide behind a pseudonym.

I'm not saying, "Don't use a pseudonym." I'm saying *don't hide* behind a pseudonym. There are good commercial or artistic reasons for writing under a pseudonym. I have a number of writer friends who use pseudonyms to "brand" their writings in different genres. For example, one well-known writer of crime thrillers adopted a pseudonym when writing a zombie horror series.

Harry Potter author J.K. Rowling is actually a pseudonym of sorts, since her legal name is Joanne Rowling and she has no middle initial. Though Rowling originally planned to use "Joanne Rowling" as her byline, the publisher convinced her to use initials instead, reasoning that boys might not read the book if they knew it was written by a woman.

In April 2013, Little Brown published Joanne Rowling's first crime novel, *The Cuckoo's Calling*, under the pseudonym "Robert Galbraith" — so, in a real sense, "Robert Galbraith" was the pseudonym of another pseudonym, "J.K. Rowling." In each case, these pseudonyms were branding decisions.

One of the most creative pseudonyms ever invented was "Lemony Snicket," which is also the name of a character in *A Series Of Unfortunate Events*, a line of popular children's books. Would the series be as popular if the author's real name, Daniel Handler, were on the cover instead of "Lemony Snicket"? Doubtful. Again, this is a branding decision.

While there are good reasons for using a pseudonym, fear is not one of them. I believe it's a *huge* mistake to write under a pseudonym out of fear of self-revelation.

Janet Flanner was an American writer who lived in Paris and wrote for *The New Yorker* for five decades. During the

1920s and '30s, she was part of a literary circle in Paris that included F. Scott Fitzgerald, Ernest Hemingway, Ezra Pound, e. e. cummings, and Gertrude Stein. Flanner was also a friend of such artists as Pablo Picasso, Georges Braque, and Henri Matisse.

Writing for *The New Yorker*, she adopted what has come to be known as "the *New Yorker* style" — a style that is witty, sophisticated, and urbane. Flanner also adopted a pseudonym, "Genêt." Ralph Keyes, in *The Courage to Write*, observes that the pseudonym made Janet Flanner "feel like an impostor." Flanner herself once said, "What I know about me I do not wish to admit. So this knowledge is canceled because of its unpleasantness. This basic evasion probably disbalances all my possibilities of self-information."[9]

In other words, Flanner deliberately and pointedly avoided self-discovery and self-revelation. She hid behind an adopted style and an affected voice, just as she hid behind a name that was not her own. She lost her style and her soul while hiding behind a pen name.

Though she spent most of her life dreaming of being a novelist, she produced only one novel in a lifetime of writing. The novel, entitled *The Cubical City*, was published in 1926 to a lukewarm reception. In 1974, when the book was reissued, Flanner penned an apologetic afterword, confessing, "I am not a first-class fiction writer as this reprinted first novel shows. Writing fiction is not my gift."

And Flanner's biographer, Brenda Wineapple, came to the same conclusion: "She feared she had ignored her inner life, preferring to skate on the surfaces of things. ... She feared she would never be able to create anything she truly respected."[10] And, in fact, Flanner never wrote another novel after *The Cubical City*.

Keyes concluded that her pseudonym, Genêt, destroyed Flanner's own original voice and her talent for writing fiction.

"After spending so much time in disguise producing literary trifles," Keyes concluded, "Flanner felt unable to shift gears and write fiction of substance. Hiding behind a pseudonym ... had allowed her to avoid the introspection and self-revelation that any serious writer must risk."[11]

If you write under a pseudonym to "brand" your work and broaden your audience, that's fine. But if you hide behind a pseudonym to disguise the truth about yourself, you could be making a terrible mistake. Janet Flanner hid behind the mask of Genêt and became a tragic figure. Come out into the open. Write your truth. Be who you are.

2. Hide in plain sight, right behind your characters.

After Junot Díaz's first novel, *The Brief Wondrous Life of Oscar Wao*, won the 2008 Pulitzer Prize for fiction, Díaz gave an interview to *Slate*'s Meghan O'Rourke. The novel describes life in the Dominican Republic under dictator Rafael Trujillo, whose oppressive rule ended with his assassination in 1961. In the interview, Díaz makes an intriguing statement: "This novel (I cannot say it enough) is all about the dangers of dictatorship — Trujillo is just the face I use to push these issues — but the real dictatorship is in the book itself, in its telling; and that's what I think is most disturbing: how deeply attached we all are to the institution of dictatorship."

When O'Rourke asked what he meant, Diaz replied, "In dictatorships, only one person is really allowed to speak. And when I write a book or a story, I too am the only one speaking, no matter how I hide behind my characters."[12]

Every writer who is truly in touch with his or her own creative process knows that this is true: We hide behind our characters. We hide behind our protagonists. We hide behind our villains. We often put words in their mouths that we don't dare speak out loud. Our characters are our masks.

And that's a good thing. That's one reason we write. If you fear revealing yourself in your writing, then let your characters speak for you.

When we tap into the unconscious mind and begin writing "in flow," our characters often seem to come alive in our imagination. It's as if they magically become independent personalities with a will all their own — a will that is separate from our own.

That, of course, is an illusion. Our characters have no existence apart from us. Though we may not consciously control our characters, we do create them, and they portray the hidden and repressed aspects of ourselves. They portray emotions, urges, hurts, rages, and fears that churn deep below the surface of our consciousness, in that vast rolling ocean of the soul, the unconscious mind.

When a character acts or speaks, we may not recognize those actions, those words, as coming from us. *But that character is us.* And when we write down a character's actions and words on the printed page, we're not just telling a story. We're revealing deep inner truths. Not all writers understand this principle — but Japanese Catholic novelist Shūsaku Endō (*The Sea and Poison*) understood it well. He said, "Over the years I have forged familial ties with these characters, who are reflections of portions of myself."[13]

One of the great advantages of being a writer of fiction is that you can, as Junot Díaz said, hide behind your characters. And hiding behind your characters is nothing more or less than hiding in plain sight. We can let our characters do our dirty work. We can let them say things we would never dare say. We can let them do the things we wouldn't be caught dead doing.

Our characters give us "plausible deniability." As Truman Capote once said, "You can't blame a writer for what the characters say." And Willa Muir, author of *Imagined Corners*, once told a reviewer, "Opinions put into the mouths of my characters are not necessarily mine."

Fiction provides the perfect cover. Your characters can say and do the most outrageous things while you feign innocence and say, "I'm just the author. I'm not responsible for what my characters do." You get to reveal yourself and hide at the same time. You can grab handfuls of slimy, wriggling nasties from the darkest recesses of your unconscious mind, dump them in the lap of your horrified reader, and say, "Hey, don't take it seriously, it's just a story. It's not real. It's just make-believe."

But you know it's *more* than that. Much more. It *is* real. It's *your* truth.

One of the best ways to hide in plain sight is to create characters who faithfully present all sides, all viewpoints, all sympathies — *and you never need to reveal which character represents you.* Make sure your hero and your villain have equally believable points of view, equally strong motivations, equally plausible worldviews. As Tolstoy observed, "A story leaves a deeper impression when it is impossible to tell which side the author is on."

Fiction provides an excellent means of exploring your own ambivalence and unresolved questions. As your characters argue their conflicting views, you can probe your own inner conflicts and grope for answers to your own questions. It's a compelling way to tell a story — and an effective way to grapple with doubts and uncertainties.

If you're afraid of revealing yourself, then hide in plain sight, right behind your characters. Become your characters, and let your characters speak for you.

3. Resist the temptation to play it safe — go for "the zone."

In Chapter 1, I discussed the experience of writing "in the zone" or "in flow." My book *Writing in Overdrive* discusses the "in the zone" process in great detail with practical step-by-step insights and examples from the lives of great writers.

Writing "in the zone" is *the* solution to *all* of our writing fears, because when we are "in the zone," we're focused totally on imagination and creativity. Emotions of self-doubt, fear, and anxiety are completely blocked out of our awareness. In "the zone," our creative process is controlled by the powerful engine of our creativity, the unconscious mind. Fear and self-doubt come from the conscious intellect, while creativity and imagination come from the unconscious. That's why "the zone" is a realm of absolute fearlessness.

When we silence our mental chatter, we calm all of our fears, including the fear of self-revelation. We stop worrying about what others think of us. We feel free to summon our deepest truth and splash it across the page. We are completely honest with ourselves and honest with the blank page, because we are in a place where there is no self-criticism, no self-awareness at all.

Writing "in the zone" produces an exuberant, emotionally intense first draft. After our "in the zone" session, we engage the conscious intellect, and we reread and revise what we have written. At that point, our conscious mind is often surprised at what the unconscious has spilled out onto the page.

Novelist Eudora Welty described her experience with an "in the zone" creative process in an interview with *The Paris Review*. She described how the writing process erased her fear of what others might think of her:

> At the time of writing, I don't write for my friends or myself, either; I write for it, for the pleasure of it. I believe if I stopped to wonder what So-and-So would think, or what I'd feel like if this were read by a stranger, I would be paralyzed. I care what my friends think, very deeply — and it's only after they've read

the finished thing that I really can rest, deep down. But in the writing, I have to just keep going straight through with only the thing in mind and what it dictates.[14]

Welty then went on to recount an incident that will be familiar to all writers who regularly write "in the zone" — the experience of reading what you have written and wondering, "Did *I* write that?" Welty talked about reading the galley proofs for her second novel, *Delta Wedding* (1946). She told the interviewer that her writing process is "so much an inward thing that reading the proofs later can be a real shock." She came upon a page of dialogue that she didn't recognize, and she thought, with absolute conviction, "I didn't write this." She was absolutely certain she had never seen that page of dialogue before. She said:

> I wrote to my editor, John Woodburn, and told him something had happened to that page in the typesetting. He was kind, not even surprised — maybe this happens to all writers. He called me up and read me from the manuscript — word for word what the proofs said. Proofs don't shock me any longer, yet there's still a strange moment with every book when I move from the position of writer to the position of reader, and I suddenly see my words with the eyes of the cold public. It gives me a terrible sense of exposure, as if I'd gotten sunburned.[15]

That sense of "sunburn" is the realization that one's hidden Self has been laid bare on the written page. That realization can come as quite a shock.

Nobel-winning novelist Saul Bellow observes that when we write freely from the unconscious mind (which he calls the "native and deeper intuitions"), the result is honest writing that flows easily and taps into the universal experiences of our readers. In a 1981 interview, he said:

> I think a writer is on-track when the door of his native and deeper intuitions is open. You write a sentence that doesn't come from that source and you can't build around it — it makes the page seem somehow false. You have a gyroscope within that tells you whether what you're doing is right or wrong. I've always felt a writer is something of a medium, and when something is really working, he has a certain clairvoyant power; he has a sense of what's going on. Whenever I've published a book that's received wide attention, I've heard from thousands of people around the world who have been thinking the same thing — as though I'd anticipated things. I didn't mean to, but I've learned one does.[16]

Writing "in the zone" is a risk. At least, it *feels* like a risk. To write "in the zone" requires that we trust the Muse, our unconscious source of creativity. And we don't like handing control over to something we don't consciously understand. We don't trust our unconscious mind. We want to assert our conscious control over the creative process.

And therein lies a much greater danger: Conscious control *destroys* the creative process. Creativity is an unconscious activity. As Carolyn Chute (*The Beans of Egypt, Maine*) observed, "Writing is like meditation or going into an ESP trance, or prayer. Like dreaming. You are tapping into your unconscious."[17]

Ralph Keyes, in *The Courage to Write*, warns us against trying to control the unconscious creative process out of a misplaced desire to play it safe:

The farther writing strays from its deepest sources, the more sterile it becomes. ... Subliminally the reader senses that the writer isn't saying what he most wants to say. He's protecting himself; being prudent. Writers realize this more consciously. One of the worst things they can say about a colleague is that he played it safe. They judge each other and themselves as much on courage and candor as on competence and craft.[18]

Writing "in the zone" silences our fears and removes our inhibitions, freeing us to reveal ourselves in our writing. The "zone" experience removes all doubt, self-criticism, and anxiety about what others may think — at least for as long as we are writing.

Once we snap out of the zone, those doubts and fears may return. But that's okay. The only thing that matters is that we were creative, productive, and fearless while we were writing. In that "zone" of protection, we are free to be who we are, free to write fearlessly.

To write courageously, freely, and brilliantly, resist the temptation to play it safe. Go for "the zone."

4. View your writing as an adventure of self-discovery.

Don't fear self-revelation — *embrace it.* You are making life-changing discoveries about yourself. You are discovering who you are, what you think, and what you believe. You're pushing back the boundaries of your ability and potential. This is the essence of adventure.

English novelist John Fowles (*The French Lieutenant's Woman*) said that, for him, writing fiction is fundamentally a journey of self-discovery:

I write fiction very much to discover myself through texts — more precisely during the process of writing them — and very little to stake a claim on the flagrant quicksand of contemporary reputation. ... My fictions are far more experiments than anything else — that is, in search of something, or things, always beyond the outward narrative and themes. This is a main reason why I find that writing ... does not get easier as I grow older.[19]

Robert Penn Warren (author of *All the King's Men*) called novels "concealed autobiography" because "you are trying to find out what you really think or who you are." And Katherine Paterson, in *The Spying Heart*, agrees: "In a real sense, I am constantly writing autobiography, but I have to turn it into fiction in order to give it credibility."

If you see writing as indecent exposure, an act of nakedly revealing your most humiliating secrets, you'll naturally be afraid of self-revelation. But if you view writing as a grand adventure, a way of unveiling the truth within, you'll look forward to the act of creation with eagerness and anticipation.

I challenge you to look at your writing with new eyes. Transmute fear into excitement. The journey of self-discovery may frighten you, but it will ultimately liberate you. It will make you a better writer, with so much more to offer your readers. As Natalie Goldberg said in *Wild Mind*, "Write what disturbs you, what you fear, what you have not been willing to speak about. ... Be willing to be split open."[20]

5. Accept the risk of self-revelation as a holy calling.

Accept the risk — or don't write.

And remember, when we talk about self-revelation, we are not talking about writing your autobiography. There are many ways you reveal yourself through your writing, and especially through your fiction.

You reveal yourself through the genre you write in, the themes you write about, the situations you create, the dialogue of your protagonists, antagonists, and secondary characters, and through your narration. If you try to hide who you are, your writing will come across as evasive, unsatisfying, and unworthy of the reader's time. "Good writers," said William Zinsser, "are visible just behind their words."

If you are unwilling or unable to write honestly, then why write at all? Why should any reader pay good money to buy your work if your work is not truthful? A decade ago, I made this statement in a book on writing:

> If you approach writing as a holy calling, you will be happy every day of your writing life, whether the money is there or not, whether the bills are paid or not, whether you are ahead of deadline or hopelessly snowed under. When writing is not just a job but a calling, nothing matters but the excellence of the work, the beauty of the words, the power of the ideas. You can block out anxiety, pressure, self-doubt, insecurity, and bill collectors, because you are following your holy calling, you are creating your holy writ, you are working holy miracles through the dance of your fingertips upon the keyboard. You are doing what you were born to do.[21]

I stand by those words today. To me, writing is still the holiest of callings, a sacred duty, a sacrament of the soul.

In a similar way, Harlan Ellison has called writing a "holy chore" — a sacred task that demands our courage and total honesty. He writes, "The chief commodity a writer has to sell is his courage. And if he has none, he is more than a coward.

He is a sellout and a fink and a heretic, because writing is a holy chore."[22]

In *Bird by Bird*, Anne Lamott reminds us that writing the truth, regardless of personal cost, is our moral obligation as writers. "Write straight into the emotional center of things," she says. "Write toward vulnerability. ... Risk being unliked. Tell the truth as you understand it. If you're a writer, you have a moral obligation to do this. And it is a revolutionary act — truth is always subversive."[23]

When we reach deep within ourselves and draw out the truth and put it on the page, we are not only writing *our* truth. We are writing *universal* truths. When our readers read what we have drawn up out of the depths of ourselves, they will say, "Here is someone who understands *me*, someone who has written *my* truth."

Writers and readers help each other not to feel alone. Ernest Hemingway put it this way in a 1934 essay for *Esquire*:

> All good books are alike in that they are truer than if they had really happened and after you are finished reading one, you will feel that all of that happened to you and afterwards it all belongs to you: the good and the bad, the ecstasy, the remorse and sorrow, the people and the places and how the weather was. If you can get so that you can give that to people, then you are a writer. Because that is the hardest thing of all to do.[24]

Writing and revealing the truth is your holy chore, your moral obligation, your secret mission, your act of subversion against an unholy world system. Don't let your reader down. Don't let yourself down. Obey your holy calling. Carry out your holy chore. Write your truth.

6. Some will condemn you. Write the truth anyway.

Once you decide to be a writer, you accept the risk of being criticized and condemned for what you write. Criticism is not a risk of writing. It's a *certainty*. If you write, someone will hate what you write. In this age of social media, people will criticize you in the most vile and offensive ways, and do so with anonymity and immunity. If you don't want to be criticized, don't write.

Some people try to protect themselves from criticism by muting their voice, softening their words, and obscuring their true meaning. Don't do it. Write clearly, boldly, and fearlessly. Use forceful, unambiguous language. State your truth in terms that cannot be misunderstood. Invite the onslaught of criticism. As Anne Lamott said, "Risk being unliked."

E. L. Doctorow said that you do your best work when you know you're transgressing other people's beliefs and stirring up criticism:

> Maybe the nature of fiction is that, unlike reporting for the *New York Times*, it has to admit everything — all aspects and forms of thought and behavior and feeling, no matter how awful they may be. Fiction has no borders, everything is open. You have a limitless possibility of knowing the truth. But there are always people telling you what you can't do, where you mustn't go. Every time you write a book, someone says, "Oh, you shouldn't have done this or you shouldn't have done that." There's always a commissar who wants to tell you what the rules are. Yet when I'm writing out of a spirit of transgression, I'm probably doing my best work.[25]

So speak the truth — but don't expect to be loved for it. As Elbert Hubbard said, the only way to avoid criticism is to "do nothing, say nothing, be nothing." When you write, expect opposition and hate. Don't go out of your way to make people angry. Don't offend for the sake of being offensive. You won't need to. The truth is offensive enough.

Expect criticism. Expect condemnation. Speak the truth anyway. Write fearlessly.

7. Extract the maximum benefit from your suffering.

Think of all the suffering in your life. Think of your most painful memories. Think of the losses and mistreatment you've suffered, the times you've been betrayed or lied to, the times life has hurt you so much you felt like giving up.

Now, think of those times as investments in your wisdom, your growth, and your writing. Don't waste that investment. Get the maximum return on every nickel's worth of suffering you've paid in. If you don't write it, you lose the benefit. So write your pain. Convert your tragedies into royalty checks. "Writing," said novelist J. P. Donleavy (*The Ginger Man*), "is turning one's worst moments into money."

In May 1934, F. Scott Fitzgerald wrote to his friend Ernest Hemingway, asking what Hemingway thought of his recently published novel, *Tender Is the Night*. Hemingway replied in a blunt yet compassionate letter.

"I liked it and I didn't," Hemingway wrote. He proceeded to describe some of the aspects of the book he didn't like. Yet he affirmed Fitzgerald's fine talent, adding, "It's a lot better than I say. But it's not as good as you can do. ... All you need to do is write truly and not care about what the fate of it is."

The centerpiece of Hemingway's advice to Fitzgerald is that he should write honestly and unflinchingly about the painfulness and injustice of life. "We are all bitched from the start," Hemingway wrote, "and you especially have to hurt like hell before you can write seriously. But when you get the damned hurt, use it — don't cheat with it. Be as faithful to it as a scientist — but don't think anything is of any importance because it happens to you or anyone belonging to you."[26]

In a video on YouTube, gothic horror novelist Anne Rice offered two guidelines for writers. The first piece of advice is a principle she learned from Floyd Salas, a Latino poet-novelist in the San Francisco Bay area. Salas told her, "Go where the pain is."

Rice explains, "What Floyd meant was, write about what hurts. Go back to the memory that causes you conflict and pain, and almost makes you unable to breathe. Write about it. Explore it in the privacy of your room, with your keyboard. Go where the pain is. Don't be afraid of that."

Her second piece of advice is a corollary to the principle she learned from Floyd Salas: "Go where the pleasure is," Rice says. "Go where you really want to be in writing. Write exciting things that you want to write. ... If you keep doing what's interesting to you, pretty soon you'll be getting out of bed in the morning and thinking, 'I've got to get to work because I want to find out what happens.'"[27]

It takes courage to follow this advice. It takes boldness to go where the pain is, to face your most hurtful memories, to dig into old wounds and dredge up old sufferings that may have been buried for years.

But if you are willing to reach inside yourself and pull out your throbbing, wounded heart and set it before the reader drenched in your own blood and tears, you'll create a piece of writing that is honest and compelling. You'll reach the reader's own place of pain, and you'll bring a light of recognition into the reader's eyes — and maybe some tears as well.

It also takes courage to go where the pleasure is. Some of us want to play it safe, to write what's current, what's popular, what we think editors are buying right now. But great writers write what they are passionate about, what they desperately want to say, and what honestly comes from deep within.

Go where the pain is, go where the pleasure is. Reveal who you are and how you experience the world. Reap the maximum return on your investment in living your life.

7. Accept self-revelation as the only path to originality.

E. B. White said, "All writing is communication; creative writing is communication through revelation — it is the Self escaping into the open." When you write to reveal yourself, when you dredge up the truth embedded in your soul, you produce work that is, by definition, original.

When you avoid the risk of self-revelation, what kind of writing are you left with? Only that which imitates others. To be original, you must write from within, from the unconscious. You must allow the Self to escape into the open and onto the page. Poet Jane Hirshfield (*Given Sugar, Given Salt*) writes:

> Passion for truth is an idea with more than one face. It includes the determination to look closely and long, to be unsatisfied with the secondhand and assumption. It includes the emotions and the body, acknowledging that the writer's whole being is the instrument of perception, not only the mind. It also hints that only the hunger for something beyond the personal will allow a writer to break free of one major obstacle to originality — the fear of self-revelation.[28]

You can't hide and be original. If you hide who you are, you write with someone else's voice, someone else's thoughts, someone else's style, someone else's truth. The writer who is fears self-revelation can only produce contrived characters, parodied stories, and a plagiarized style. Look within and find your own original truth — then fling your truth onto the page for the whole world to see.

Don't defraud yourself and your readers. Write the stories and books that only you can write. Be who you are. Write fearlessly.

---

1. Maria Popova, "Why I Write: Joan Didion on Ego, Grammar & the Impetus to Create," BrainPickings.org, October 16, 2012, http://www.brainpickings.org/index.php/2012/10/16/why-i-write-joan-didion/.

2. Donald Morison Murray, *Shoptalk: Learning to Write with Writers* (Portsmouth, NH: Boynton/Cook Publishers, 1990), 72.

3. Barbara Abercrombie, *A Year of Writing Dangerously: 365 Days of Inspiration & Encouragement* (Novato, CA: New World Library, 2012), 5.

4. Ibid, emphasis in the original.

5. Farhat Iftekharuddin, Joseph Boyden, Mary Rohrberger, and Jale Claudet, *The Postmodern Short Story: Forms and Issues* (Westport, CT: Praeger, 2003), 170; cf. E. L. Doctorow, "E. L. Doctorow Quotes," GoodReads.com, http://www.goodreads.com/author/quotes/12584.E_L_Doctorow.

6. Harlan Ellison, "Ellison Quotes and Anecdotes," HarlanEllison.com, http://harlanellison.com/quotes.htm.

7. Bernie S. Siegel, MD, "Writing as Surgery: Words and Swords," *Virtual Mentor*, American Medical Association Journal of Ethics, October 2004, http://virtualmentor.ama-assn.org/2004/10/mhum1-0410.html.

8. Lucas Matthiessen, Willie Morris, John Marquand, "Irwin Shaw, The Art of Fiction No. 4 (Continued)," *The Paris Review*, Spring 1979, http://www.theparisreview.org/interviews/3395/the-art-of-fiction-no-4-continued-irwin-shaw.

9. Ralph Keyes, *The Courage to Write: How Writers Transcend Fear* (New York: Macmillan, 2003), 69-70, emphasis in the original.

10. Ibid.

11. Ibid.

12. Meghan O'Rourke, "Questions for Junot Díaz," *Slate*, April 8, 2008, http://www.slate.com/articles/news_and_politics/recycled/2008/04/questions_for_junot_daz.html.

13. David Clive Price, "On Thin Ice," review of *The Final Martyrs* by Shūsaku Endō, *Far Eastern Economic Review*, February 24, 1994, 37.

14. Linda Kuehl, "Eudora Welty, The Art of Fiction No. 47," *The Paris Review*, Fall 1972, http://www.theparisreview.org/interviews/4013/the-art-of-fiction-no-47-eudora-welty.

15. Ibid.

16. Gloria L. Cronin and Ben Siegel, editors, *Conversations with Saul Bellow* (Jackson, MS: University Press of Mississippi, 1994), 188.

17. The New York Times, *Writers on Writing: Collected Essays from The New York Times* (New York: Times Books/Holt, 2001), 38.

18. Ralph Keyes, *The Courage to Write: How Writers Transcend Fear* (New York: Henry Holt, 1995), 71.

19. John Fowles, "Foreword," in Harald William Fawkner's *The Timescapes of John Fowles* (Cranbury, NJ: Associated University Presses, 1984), 9.

20. Natalie Goldberg, *Wild Mind: Living the Writer's Life* (New York: Bantam, 1990), 71.

21. Jim Denney, *Quit Your Day Job!: How to Sleep Late, Do What You Enjoy, and Make a Ton of Money as a Writer* (Sanger, CA: Quill Driver Books, 2004), 13-14.

22. Harlan Ellison, ed., *Dangerous Visions* (Garden City, NY: Doubleday, 1967), 171.

23. Anne Lamott, *Bird by Bird: Some Instructions on Writing and Life* (New York: Anchor, 1995), 226.

24. Jerry W. Knudson, *In the News: American Journalists View Their Craft* (Wilmington, DE: Scholarly Resources, 2000), 209.

25. Christopher D. Morris, ed., *Conversations with E. L. Doctorow* (Jackson, MS: University Press of Mississippi, 1999), 87.

26. Shaun Usher, "Forget Your Personal Tragedy," LettersOfNote.com, April 25, 2012, http://www.lettersofnote.com/2012/04/forget-your-personal-tragedy.html.

27. Anne Rice, "Anne Gives Writing Advice 09.18.12," YouTube video, posted by Anne Rice, transcribed by Jim Denney, http://www.youtube.com/watch?v=bw2KXX7WrOY&feature=player_embedded#at=356.

28. Jane Hirshfield, *Nine Gates: Entering the Mind of Poetry* (New York: Harper, 1997), 38.

Fear No. 6
"I'm Afraid of Rejection"

———

"Rejection slips
are lacerations of the soul,
if not quite inventions
of the devil — but there is no
way around them."
Isaac Asimov

———

You are undoubtedly familiar with the accomplishments of the Brontë sisters, Charlotte (*Jane Eyre*), Emily (*Wuthering Heights*), and Anne (*The Tenant of Wildfell Hall*). These three sisters produced many enduring literary classics.

But there was another Brontë whose name might not be as familiar: Patrick Branwell Brontë, the brother of the three Brontë sisters. The four Brontë siblings were inseparable in their early years. As children, they engaged in fantasy role-playing games and collaborated on complex stories about an imaginary realm they called Angria.

As an adult, Branwell often talked about the grand novel he intended to write. But while his sisters produced their literary masterpieces, Branwell dabbled at writing. He thought writing should come easily, and he once told a friend about his dream of making "a name in the world of posterity, without being pestered by the small but countless botherments ... of work-day toil."[1]

Branwell's sisters had read the few fragments of the novel he had started, and they thought his natural talent for writing far outshone theirs. They urged him to show a few pages of his work-in-progress to a publisher, but Branwell refused, saying he couldn't bear the thought of an editor tossing his writings into the fireplace.

It's a mystery why Branwell thought an editor would burn his manuscript. His fear of rejection was way out of proportion to reality. Though he wrote only sporadically and refused to submit his work to a publisher, he continued bragging to his friends about the novel that would one day bring him fame and fortune — in his dreams.

In the fall of 1848, Branwell Brontë fell gravely ill with tuberculosis, aggravated by delirium tremens from alcoholism. He died on September 24 at age thirty-one. After Branwell's funeral, Charlotte Brontë wrote of her brother, "I do not weep from a sense of bereavement ... but for the wreck of talent, the ruin of promise, the untimely dreary extinction of what might have been a burning and shining light."[2]

Branwell Brontë died in despair, knowing he had wasted his life and his talent. He never wrote his grand novel. Why? *Because he was terrified of rejection.* His irrational fear of rejection prevented him from setting down his literary vision on paper and submitting it to a publisher. His were the same fears many writers face today.

As fantasy novelist Laurell K. Hamilton observes, "A writer writes. I've lost track of the number of people who want to be writers but never actually write anything. Talking about writing ... won't get a book written. You've got to write."[3]

I believe that writers who write fearlessly usually enjoy successful careers. Writers who allow themselves to be ruled by fear risk ending their lives in despair and obscurity — just like Branwell Brontë. Don't waste your life and your talent. Don't be paralyzed by the fear of rejection. Conquer fear. Live the life you dream of — the life of a successful writer.

The story that only you can write

Why do writers fear rejection?

Many aspiring writers seem perfectly at ease showing their writings to friends, fellow writers, professors, and Mom and Dad. But the thought of putting a manuscript in an envelope and mailing it off to an editor fills some writers with terror.

Many of us, it seems, are afraid that the gatekeepers of the publishing world — editors — will condemn our work, and us with it. But rejection is not a terrifying calamity that randomly invades a writer's life. Rejection is *the inevitable and ever-present reality* of the writer's life. No serious writer escapes rejection. The writer's road is paved with rejection.

A writer who fears rejection is like a surgeon who fears the sight of blood or a symphony conductor who can't stand violin music. If you fear rejection, why would you ever choose to be a writer?

A writer must write. If you submit your work to editors, you will be rejected more often than you will be accepted. What do you do when your manuscript comes back with a rejection slip? You mail it off to the next editor in line, and you keep writing. Neil Gaiman says a writer needs a "crazed ego that doesn't allow for failure," and adds:

The best reaction to a rejection slip is a sort of wild-eyed madness, an evil grin, and sitting yourself in front of the keyboard muttering, "Okay, you bastards.

Try rejecting *this*!" and then writing something so unbelievably brilliant that all other writers will disembowel themselves with their pens upon reading it, because there's nothing left to write.[4]

Novelist John Scalzi says that aspiring writers often ask him, "What if I send something out and it gets rejected?" He replies:

> What do you mean "*if*"?
> Take this now and engrave this in your brain: *EVERY WRITER GETS REJECTED. You will be no different.* ... The editor is not rejecting you as a human being or your right to exist on this planet. He or she is merely rejecting an article you've submitted. That's all. That's it.
> If you can't handle the idea of rejection, you're really in the wrong line of work. It's just part of the business.[5]

Ray Bradbury told his biographer Sam Weller about the first (and only) time he sold a short story to *The New Yorker.* In 1947, he got a letter from Katharine Angell, the literary editor of *The New Yorker* (and, incidentally, the wife of novelist E. B. White). Bradbury had never submitted to the publication before and had never had any prior contact with Mrs. Angell. She wrote, "I've read your short stories recently in several magazines. Do you have anything you can send to *The New Yorker?*"

Bradbury had a story called "I See You Never," about an illegal immigrant from Mexico who was being deported. The story had been rejected by dozens of magazines. Bradbury sent Angell the manuscript, and she accepted it and paid $300 — the most money Bradbury had yet received for one story.

"It was my first sale to *The New Yorker*," Bradbury told Weller, "and I never made another one. Thirty years went by, and they rejected hundreds of my stories."[6] Bradbury often said that he held the record for the most stories rejected by *The New Yorker*.

Ray Bradbury never feared rejection. He talked about rejection slips as if they were memories of severe weather — "the great blizzard of rejection slips of 1935 ... the snowstorm of rejection slips in '37 and '38."[7] In his classic instruction book for writers, *Zen in the Art of Writing*, Bradbury explains why the key to surviving rejection is to write your own self-revealing story, the story that only you can write:

> There is only one type of story in the world. Your story. If you write your story it could possibly sell to any magazine.
>
> I have had stories rejected by *Weird Tales* that I turned around and sold to *Harper's*.
>
> I have had stories rejected by *Planet Stories* that I sold to *Mademoiselle*.
>
> Why? Because I have always tried to write my own story. Give it a label if you wish, call it science fiction or fantasy or the mystery or the western. But, at heart, all good stories are the one kind of story, the story written by an individual man from his individual truth. That kind of story can be fitted into any magazine, be it the *Post* or *McCall's, Astounding Science-Fiction, Harper's Bazaar*, or *The Atlantic*.[8]

If you are afraid of rejection, you must face your fear and do the thing that frightens you. You have to write, you have to submit your writing to an editor, you have to wait for the editor to report back, and yes, you have to endure the momentary sting of rejection. And you have to do it again and again and again.

But every time you attempt something challenging and you get through it, you ratchet your confidence up one more notch. That's why Ralph Waldo Emerson said, "Do the thing you fear, and the death of fear is certain."

Let me suggest a few principles to help get you through the times of rejection — and get you to that long-awaited moment of celebration when you make that sale.

1. Never accept rejection as final.

Novelist-playwright William Saroyan spent one full year writing stories, submitting them to every paying market in the country, and receiving nothing but rejection slips. Yet Saroyan refused to accept rejection as final. He took his stack of manuscripts, which had already been rejected by every magazine in existence, and he sent them out again — *to the very same markets that had already rejected them.*

The second time around, his stories began to sell. The reason they sold was that there is a high turnover rate among junior editors who read the slush piles. By the time Saroyan sent his manuscripts back to the same magazines, the people who had rejected them had moved on. A whole new round of junior editors began reading — and liking — his stories.

Science fiction writer Frank Herbert spent five years researching, writing, and revising a sprawling novel about interplanetary intrigue and Machiavellian conspiracies on a desert planet called *Dune*. Herbert sold the serial rights to *Analog* magazine. *Analog* divided Herbert's novel into two sections, then serialized each section, the first part in 1963, the second part in 1965. Herbert then reworked and expanded the novel and submitted it for publication in book form. At that point, he ran into a stone wall of rejection.

Dune was rejected by more than twenty publishing houses — all the leading houses that published in the science fiction genre. Refusing to concede defeat, Herbert began submitting *Dune* to publishers that had never published science fiction before, including Chilton Books, a small publisher that specialized in car repair manuals. In one of the strangest and luckiest publishing decisions ever made, Chilton accepted *Dune*, paying Herbert a pittance of an advance.

Dune quickly found an eager audience — and it went on to win the Hugo and Nebula Awards for best novel. The book has remained continuously in print ever since, and is the best-selling science fiction novel of all time. It has spawned an entire franchise, including sequels, motion picture adaptations, and merchandise.

The moral of the story: Never accept rejection as final. Keep writing and submitting and one day you will sell. As Lawrence Block advises, "Once you've got a story to the point where you think it's worth submitting, you must submit it and submit it and submit it until someone somewhere breaks down and buys it."[9]

2. Obey Heinlein's rules for writers.

Robert A. Heinlein, author of *Starship Troopers* and *Stranger in a Strange Land*, once said, "Writers — including scarred old professionals — are inordinately fond of their brainchildren. They would rather see their firstborn child ravaged by wolves than suffer the pain of having a manuscript rejected. So instead they read their manuscripts aloud to spouses and long-suffering friends."[10]

To help writers find relief from the fear of rejection, Heinlein formulated five rules for writing success. Another great science-fiction writer, Robert J. Sawyer, posted Heinlein's five rules on his website, and added a sixth rule of his own. Here are Heinlein's — and Sawyer's — rules for overcoming rejection and finding success as a writer:

Rule One: *You Must Write*. This seems obvious, but it's amazing how many aspiring writers never seem to get around to actually writing. If you're going to be a writer, you must inscribe words that other people will pay money to read.

Rule Two: *Finish What You Start*. Again, this seems so basic it goes without saying. Yet many writers (and I include my early self in this) seem to falter somewhere around the halfway to three-quarters mark. We run out of steam. We run out of motivation. We get blocked. We set aside one book to chase some sparkly new idea. Heinlein reminds us: You can't be a writer unless you discipline yourself to finish what you start.

Rule Three: *You Must Refrain From Rewriting, Except to Editorial Order*. Heinlein is not saying you should turn in your raw first draft. If you care about your art, you will carefully, painstakingly do a second and third draft. Maybe even a fourth. But then it's time to stop, print out your story, put it in an envelope, and send it to an editor. Resist the obsessive-compulsive temptation to tinker *ad infinitum, ad nauseum*, with your story. Be done with it, and start on your *next* story.

If your story is rejected by one editor, don't assume it is hopelessly flawed and mut be completely rewritten. Rejection doesn't mean your story is "bad." Rejection only means "this story is not what we're looking for right now," or even, "our assistant editor didn't have the brains to see what a brilliant story you've written." If your story is rejected by one editor, immediately send out to the next. Keep submitting it until it sells or you've completely exhausted the market — but resist the temptation to tinker with it between submissions.

If an editor asks you for revisions, either after a sale or as a condition of acceptance, then by all means, revise away! Give the editor what he or she asks for. But until then, treat your manuscript as if it were carved in stone. Don't change a word of it.

Rule Four: *You Must Put Your Story on the Market.* This is what separates a professional writer from a dabbler. To put your story on the market is to submit it to an editor. You're not writing to amuse yourself. You're writing for publication. Make a serious, determined effort to get your story published.

Rule Five: *You Must Keep It on the Market until It Has Sold.* After you submit your story to an editor, it will probably be rejected. When it comes back with a rejection slip, take the manuscript out of the old envelope, put it in a new envelope, and send it out to another editor the very same day. That's what it means to keep a story on the market until it has sold.

Finally, there is Robert J. Sawyer's additional rule:

Rule Six: *Start Working on Something Else.* Sawyer goes on to explain: "As soon as you've finished one piece, start on another. Don't wait for the first story to come back from the editor you've submitted it to; get to work on your next project. ... You must produce a body of work to count yourself as a real working pro. ... If you have at least a modicum of talent and if you live by these six rules, you will make it."[11]

3. Beware of Teresa Nielsen Hayden's deal-breakers.

Teresa Nielsen Hayden is a writer and consulting editor for Tor Books. In a 2004 blog post, she explained the process of accepting and rejecting manuscripts at Tor. The vast majority of manuscripts, she said, can be dispatched with a "fast reject." Editors and slush pile readers can easily size up a manuscript based on fourteen attributes. Thirteen of these fourteen attributes are fatal to acceptance — they are deal-breakers. In fact, up to 75 percent of manuscripts can be rejected after a quick glance at the manuscript, because one or more of the first seven attributes can be spotted immediately.

Let's start with the first seven of Teresa Nielsen Hayden's deal-breakers (which I have paraphrased and condensed):

1. The author appears functionally illiterate.

2. The author has submitted a novel in a genre that the publisher doesn't publish.

3. The author is afflicted with "a serious neurochemical disorder," resulting in such mannerisms as the use of ALL-CAPITAL LETTERS for emphasis, and ignoring formatting standards for margins.

4. The author shows a poor grasp of English usage and sentence structure. Examples include using the wrong words (for example, "reeking havoc" instead of "wreaking havoc") and sentences written with events out of chronological order ("'Hello, John,' Mary said after she opened the door and saw John standing on the porch").

5. The author can write basic sentences, but is not able to combine them into logically ordered paragraphs.

6. The author has "a moderate neurochemical disorder" as evidenced by a confusing habit of abruptly changing subjects.

7. The author's story is intelligible but dull and pointless.

Any one of these seven problems can be spotted almost instantly, and will doom a manuscript to rejection in seconds. Again, three-quarters of all submissions are quickly eliminated on the basis of one or more of these seven characteristics.

The next seven characteristics are less obvious and take more time to spot. Hayden says that almost all of an editor's reading time is devoted to determining whether or not the few remaining manuscripts contain the next seven characteristics:

8. The author appears to be working out some deep-seated emotional issues, and should do so in therapy, not in a novel.

9. The plot of this novel is so "dull" and "flaccid" that no reader will care about this "underperforming" book.

10. The book has an engaging plot, but only because it is an unoriginal reworking of a popular movie or novel.

109

If the editor encounters characteristics 8, 9, or 10, the manuscript will be rejected. Now we come to attributes found in the top 1 to 5 percent of manuscripts in the slush pile:

11. The book is competently written and publishable — but it does not excite the editors. "Someone could publish this book," the editors say, "but we don't see why it should be us."

12. The author is talented and shows promise, but this particular book is the wrong book to serve as a launching pad for the author's career.

13. It's a well-written book, but the editors know that the marketing team and other decision-makers won't get behind this kind of book.

Finally, there is this characteristic:

14. The editor is entertained and spellbound. After eagerly reading the book from start to finish, the editor says, "Sold!"

Hayden concludes that if you want to end up in category 14, simply write a book filled with surprises and delights — the kind of book that keeps the reader turning pages until the very end.[12] That's the *only* way to avoid a rejection slip.

4. View rejection as feedback, not failure.

British mystery writer Alex Keegan is the author of numerous novels, including *Cuckoo*, *Razorbill*, and *A Wild Justice*. A number of years ago, Keegan made a careful study of the submission and rejection process, and he realized that a writer who consistently attacks the markets will develop *a predictable ratio of sales to rejections.*

"It's a fact," Keegan said, "that the more you submit, the more you will be rejected, but ... [you] cannot fail if you work at your art, if you read, read, read, write, write, write, submit, submit, submit."

He started a boot camp consisting largely of unpublished fiction writers. Of the eleven founding members, eight had no publishing credits at all. He set tough rules for membership. Each writer had to commit to producing a short story every two weeks. The group would critique it, then the writer would revise it and submit it for publication.

During the first year of the group's existence, all eleven writers made sales — a total of eighty-five stories sold. One writer won the BBC World Service's Short Story of the Year award. Keegan himself sold a novel and forty short pieces.

The group stayed together, racking up two hundred sales in the second year. The third year, three hundred fifty sales. Sales snowballed as a result of the ever-increasing number of submissions.

More submissions meant more rejections. After the boot camp's first year, Keegan said, "I had more rejections than in the previous forty-nine years of my life. But rejections are side effects, meaningless. ... I kept my belief in myself, my work."

Keegan charted his submissions on a spreadsheet and was able to calculate a "hit rate" — a ratio based on the number of sales per submissions. By rapidly submitting story after story, he developed a consistent "hit rate" of one sale for every three and a half submissions.

Because he now knew that he had a dependable "batting average," Keegan could view rejections as feedback instead of failure. He knew that every rejection slip brought him another step closer to a sale. He concluded, "I can count. I know that three rejections mean a sale. I welcome rejections. ... I eat rejections like Popeye eats spinach."[13]

This mindset is the key to unlocking the fear of rejection. If you keep writing and keep submitting, you'll eventually see that you, too, have a consistent "batting average"—

And you'll know that rejection is nothing to fear.

1. Francis A. Leyland, *The Brontë Family*, Volume 2 (London: Hurst and Blackett, 1886), 173, http://www.gutenberg.org/files/37844/37844-h/37844-h.htm.

2. Helene Moglen, *Charlotte Brontë: The Self Conceived* (Madison: University of Wisconsin Press, 1984), 77.

3. Michael McCarty, *More Giants of the Genre* (Rockville, MD: Wildside Press, 2005), 25.

4. Neil Gaiman, "On Writing," Neil Gaiman's Journal, February 3, 2004, http://journal.neilgaiman.com/2004/02/on-writing.asp.

5. John Scalzi, "John Scalzi's Utterly Useless Writing Advice," Whatever.Scalzi.com, December 17, 2004, http://whatever.scalzi.com/2004/12/17/john-scalzis-utterly-useless-writing-advice/.

6. Sam Weller, *Listen to the Echoes: The Ray Bradbury Interviews* (Brooklyn: Melville House, 2010), 114.

7. Maria Popova, "Ray Bradbury on Facing Rejection ... and Being Inspired by Snoopy," *The Atlantic*, May 21, 2012, http://www.theatlantic.com/entertainment/archive/2012/05/ray-bradbury-on-facing-rejection-and-being-inspired-by-snoopy/257478/.

8. Ray Bradbury, *Zen in the Art of Writing: Releasing the Creative Genius Within You* (New York: Bantam, 1992), 136.

9. Lawrence Block, *Telling Lies for Fun and Profit* (New York: Morrow, 1981), 58.

10. Robert A. Heinlein, "Guest Editorial," *Analog Science Fiction/Science Fact*, January 1974, 7.

11. Robert J. Sawyer, "On Writing — Heinlein's Rules," SFWriter.com, 1996, http://www.sfwriter.com/ow05.htm.

12. Teresa Nielsen Hayden, "Slushkiller," Making Light blog, February 2, 2004, http://nielsenhayden.com/makinglight/archives/004641.html.

13. Alex Keegan, "Dealing with Rejection," Writers Write: The Internet Writing Journal, October 1998, http://www.writerswrite.com/journal/oct98/keegan12.htm.

Fear No. 7
"I'm Afraid I Might Fail"

———

"You fail only if you stop writing."
Ray Bradbury

———

In 1983, Margaret Atwood rented a fisherman's cottage in the English seacoast village of Blakeney, Norfolk. She planned to spend the next six months writing her most ambitious novel yet — a complex and richly detailed dystopian tale.

Atwood soon realized she was unable to write. The sheer scope of her novel intimidated her. She spent her days bird-watching and her nights reading bad historical novels and nursing chilblains caused by the cold damp weather. She later referred to that time as "six months of futile striving."

What was wrong? Why didn't she write? Answer: She was blocked by fear of failure. Her vision of the novel loomed so large in her mind that she felt overwhelmed and paralyzed. She didn't know where to begin.

Frustrated with herself for wasting months of valuable writing time, Atwood finally did what every successful writer *must* do in order to overcome the fear of failure: *She wrote.* She began producing bits and pieces of the story. She sketched

113

in characters and wrote patches of dialogue. It didn't all hang together at first, but that didn't matter. After six months, she was finally *writing* again.

"I grasped the nettle I had been avoiding," she later said, "and began to write *The Handmaid's Tale.*" That novel later became her most successful and acclaimed work. Her advice to anyone who is paralyzed by the fear of failure: "Get back on the horse that threw you, as they used to say. They also used to say: you learn as much from failure as you learn from success."[1]

This was hardly Margaret Atwood's first novel. She had already enjoyed a fifteen-year, five-novel career when she found herself blocked during *The Handmaid's Tale.* So the fear of failure is *not* restricted to beginning and aspiring writers. Successful novelists often experience this fear as well. Like Margaret Atwood, you can conquer your fear of failure and go on to achieve your greatest work.

The conquest of this fear begins with acceptance of the inevitability of failure. The writer's life is riddled with failures of every kind and description. To write is to know failure. Most writers experience more failure than success, and we all strive to achieve what is probably unattainable.

Irish novelist Anne Enright describes a frustration most writers have felt — that of always aspiring to an artistic goal that is just beyond our reach: "I still have this big, stupid idea that if you are good enough and lucky enough, you can make an object that insists on its own subjective truth, a personal thing, a book that shifts between its covers and will not stay easy on the page, a real novel, one that lives, talks, breathes, and refuses to die. And in this, I am doomed to fail."[2]

And English novelist Will Self said, "To attempt to write seriously is always, I feel, to fail. The disjunction between my beautifully sonorous, accurate and painfully affecting mental content and the leaden, halting sentences on the page always seems a dreadful falling short. ... I prize this sense of failure — embrace it even."[3]

The writing life can be hard on friendships and family relationships. Non-writers rarely understand a writer's time pressures and his or her need to guard writing time against interruptions. And non-writers are frequently exasperated by their writer friends because they don't understand that *writers are always writing.*

Humorist James Thurber once said, "I never quite know when I'm not writing. Sometimes my wife comes up to me at a party and says, 'Dammit, Thurber, stop writing.' She usually catches me in the middle of a paragraph. Or my daughter will look up from the dinner table and ask, 'Is he sick?' 'No,' my wife says, 'he's writing something.'"[4]

Novelist Kristin Bair O'Keeffe, author of *Thirsty,* coined a term that describes a writer's usual mental state: *writerhead.* She defines writerhead as "a (usually) temporary state of dreamy concentration and fluctuating consciousness during which a writer feels most creative, productive, and artistic." She offers an example of the use of the term in a sentence: "Sssshhhh, I'm in writerhead."[5]

Your friends do not have to understand your writerhead, but they must at least tolerate it, or the friendship is doomed. I have lost more than one friendship because a friend could not tolerate who and what I am as a writer.

As Will Self has said, "To continue writing is to accept failure as simply a part of the experience."[6] As writers, we have to accept the inevitability of commercial failure, artistic failure, and even failed relationships.

If you have a morbid fear of failure, then don't write. No writer succeeds at everything, all the time. For better or worse, a certain amount of failure just comes with the territory.

"Fail early, fail often"

The fear of failure afflicts many writers soon after the publication of their first book. The writer thinks, "I fooled 'em once, but can I fool 'em again? What if I only have one book in me? What if I have no encore?"

Suspense writer James L. Rubart, author of *Rooms* and *Book of Days*, recalls that after his first book was well-received by critics and readers, he worried that it was a fluke — and that his second novel might not measure up. "The response to *Rooms* was so strong that I was definitely nervous when *Book of Days* came out. That whole 'I only have one book in me' thing. But a lot of people liked *Book of Days* better."

In fact, Rubart says, his mastery of the writing craft increased in demonstrable ways with each new novel. "It took me six years to write *Rooms*," he recalls, "two years to write *Book of Days*, five months to write *The Chair*, ten weeks to write *Soul's Gate* ... and I'm on pace to finish the novel I'm working on right now in six weeks."[7]

Wendell Berry is a farmer, antiwar activist, novelist, and poet. He remembers the sense of unease he felt after his first book was published. He has learned to embrace that uneasy feeling and to anticipate the unknown adventures ahead. "I am discomforted," he says, "by the knowledge that I don't know how to write the books that I have not yet written. But that discomfort has an excitement about it, and it is the necessary antecedent of one of the best kinds of happiness."[8]

In *A Moveable Feast*, Ernest Hemingway recalled the twinge of self-doubt he felt as he contemplated a new story:

> I would stand and look out over the roofs of Paris and think, "Do not worry. You have always written before and you will write now. All you have to do is

write one true sentence. Write the truest sentence you know." So finally I would write one true sentence, and then go on from there. It was easy then because there was always one true sentence that you knew or had seen or had heard someone say.[9]

Don't fear that you have no more stories or books in you. You have barely scratched the surface of all the stories your soul contains. Over time, you have learned and grown as a writer. Relax in the confidence and mastery you have gained from that achievement — and prepare to conquer even greater challenges in the future. Trust your Muse, your unconscious mind, your talent, your training, and your experience. Then sit down in front of your screen or your blank page, and write the truest sentence you know.

Web writer Diogenes Brito says that he wrestles with a number of fears every time he sets out to write — fear of the blank page, fear of the unknown, fear of being judged, and fear of losing control. But one fear that no longer troubles him is the fear of failure. Brito says he overcame that fear thanks to one of his university professors:

When I was in Stanford's design program, a professor named Dave Beach had everyone raise jazz hands to the sky. He then instructed us to jump and cheer, "I failed!" I have never forgotten that moment. "Fail early, fail often" was the mantra. The goal was to build up an immunity to failure, so that fear of it would never hold you back. Like [computer scientist] Dick Karpinski says, "Anything worth doing is worth doing badly — at first." I remember that, and it keeps me from freezing up. The enemy of creativity is fear, so I keep going, no matter what.[10]

If you live by the maxim, "Fail early, fail often," you can write without fear of failure. Train yourself to view failure not as an objective reality but as a false label people impose on a learning experience. Instead of telling yourself, "How horrible — I've failed," simply shrug and say, "Well, *that* didn't work. Lesson learned. What should I try next?" Make up your mind to learn from your failures and you'll stop being afraid.

Here are some suggestions to help you to overcome your fear of failure, once and for all:

1. Be bold, dare to fail, take creative risks.

In her haunting novel *Suspicion*, Barbara Rogan tells the story of Emma Roth, a novelist whose dream house becomes a house of horrors. Early in the novel, there's a scene in which Emma discusses her latest novel, a ghost story, with her agent. "Was the last book too like the one before?"

The agent hesitates. "Okay, sure," she says. "I'd like to see you push the envelope, grow as a writer. But ... consistency's a real virtue when you're trying to build a solid base of readers."

Emma isn't satisfied with that answer. She realizes that she doesn't admire "consistency" in other writers. "Prison bars are consistent, pudding is consistent," she thinks. In other words, consistency is boring. Who does Emma admire? Writers who "take risks, try things, dare to fail now and then."[11]

And I would guess that the writers *you* admire most are the ones who take daring risks for their art. Do you have the courage to get up there and walk the tightrope with the writers you admire?

If all you care about is commercial success, then there's a lot to be said for consistency, for playing it safe, for avoiding risk. But if you want to succeed artistically, if you aspire to fulfill your potential as a writer, you must overcome your fear of failure. Screenwriter Robert McKee put it this way:

Write every day, line by line, page by page, hour by hour. Do this despite fear. For above all else, beyond imagination and skill, what the world asks of you is courage, courage to risk rejection, ridicule and failure. As you follow the quest for stories told with meaning and beauty, study thoughtfully but write boldly. Then, like the hero of the fable, your dance will dazzle the world.[12]

Or, as T.S. Eliot put it, "Only those who risk going too far can possibly find out how far one can go."

2. Embrace your fear; write anyway.

In *Writing to Save Your Life*, Michele Weldon suggests a written exercise to help you identify your fears and overcome them. She suggests you make a written list of all your fears. Next to each fear, write down how that fear affects your life. Does it cause you to procrastinate? Does it keep you from starting? Does it cause you to abandon your project without finishing it? Does it cause you to censor yourself and play it safe as a writer?

Next, look over your list and ask yourself, "Which of these fears comes from me, from my own neurotic self-doubt — and which of these fears have been taught to me or imposed on me by others?" Recognizing the true source of our fears can place them in a more realistic perspective.

Now ask yourself: What is the possibility of these fears coming true? What's the worst that can happen if they do? Suppose you fail — what then? Would it be the end of the world or would you continue writing?

Finally, go down the list of your fears and, next to each fear, write these words: "I will write anyway." Make that your solemn commitment, then keep that commitment every day. No matter what you fear, no matter what may happen, write anyway.

Michele Weldon also suggests that you have a plan for those times when the fear seems especially strong. Anytime you feel the fear begin to interfere with your writing, be ready to call a friend, a therapist, or a clergy member who can talk you down from the ledge of your fear. "Tell yourself that you will do your best," Weldon concludes, "and it is good enough. It is all you need to do. It is perfect."[13]

Don't let your fears to interfere with your writing. If you fail, you fail — and you can still keep going. There's life after failure. (Take it from someone who's failed many times.) As psychiatrist David Viscott has said, "If you could get up the courage to begin, you have the courage to succeed."

3. To avoid failure, never be dull.

An interviewer once asked Elmore Leonard — author of *Glitz*, *Get Shorty*, and other fast-paced detective fiction — why his books were so popular. Leonard replied, "I leave out the parts that people skip."[14] The writer who is never dull will never lack readers. Grab your reader by the throat on the first page — then don't let go. Don't give your reader any excuse to put the book down. Make your writing as addictive as a narcotic. Sustain your intensity throughout the book.

One way to make sure your writing is fast-paced and addictive is by ruthless cutting when you rewrite. As a general rule, your second draft should almost always be shorter than your first. The lone exception to the rule is when, in your second draft, you layer in additional story material, such as a subplot or two.

There is always material that can and should be cut in the rewrite stage. There are always passages in your early drafts that readers will skip. Ruthlessly cut the skippable parts of your book in the rewrite stage. If your novel keeps getting longer with each rewrite, you're doing something wrong.

A few years ago, I wrote a series of science-fantasy novels for young readers. When I contracted the series, I submitted plot outlines for each book, and I estimated each plot to be the equivalent of a 60,000-word novel. The editors said they wanted each book to be 35,000 words long.

I decided to write them according to my original concept. If they came out too long, I'd cut them in rewrite. Sure enough, my first draft of each book came in at about 50,000 to 60,000 words. In rewrite, I went through each book and cut sentence by sentence, even word by word, sculpting each book down to the contracted 35,000-word limit. I never cut an entire scene. I simply compressed the original story into a more condensed space. The result? A fast-paced, exciting story — and a lot of enthusiastic fan mail.

Many writers make the mistake of falling in love with their words. They can't stand to see their lovely words deleted. But as mystery writer Nora DeLoach so wisely said, "If you fall in love with the vision you want of your work and not your words, the rewriting will become easier."

The specific words don't matter nearly as much as your vision for the work. After the tale is told, the reader will not remember the beauty of your prose. The reader will remember scenes and characters, emotions and images. Be willing to cut words in order to make your story and characters more vivid and memorable. Do this — and you will have no need to be afraid of failure.

4. Consciously, intentionally decide to make mistakes.

In an interview, Kristin Bair O'Keeffe described how she went from fear to fearlessness as a writer: "So many things used to scare me. ... I was afraid of reading my work out loud, speaking in front of groups, writing the stories I really wanted to write, revealing (mostly to myself) what I was truly interested in. ... But screw fear. Fear sucks. It's fake. It's man-made. It's self-perpetuated. ... *I eat fear!*"[15]

O'Keeffe credits novelist Neil Gaiman for the key insight that dispelled her many fears. She quotes from Gaiman's New Year's Eve 2011 blog post:

> I hope that in this year to come, you make mistakes.
>
> Because if you are making mistakes, then you are making new things, trying new things, learning, living, pushing yourself, changing yourself, changing your world. You're doing things you've never done before, and more importantly, you're Doing Something.
>
> So that's my wish for you, and all of us, and my wish for myself. Make New Mistakes. Make glorious, amazing mistakes. Make mistakes nobody's ever made before. Don't freeze, don't stop, don't worry that it isn't good enough, or it isn't perfect, whatever it is: art, or love, or work, or family, or life.
>
> Whatever it is you're scared of doing, Do it.[16]

Gaiman's words inspired O'Keeffe's writing mantra "I eat fear!"[17] This is wise practical advice for any writer who fears failure: Make up your mind that you will make some glorious, amazing mistakes. Attempt the impossible. Fail spectacularly. In the process, you'll have more fun than you ever dreamed possible. Throw out your inhibitions, set off your imagination like a Roman candle, and reach for the stars.

Learn by failing. Grow wise by making mistakes. Fear will have no hold on you, because you will have nothing to fear.

So say it aloud: "I eat fear."

Louder! *"I EAT FEAR!"*
Now write — and *write fearlessly.*

---

1. Margaret Atwood, "Falling Short: Seven Writers Reflect on Failure," *The Guardian*, June 22, 2013, http://m.guardian.co.uk/books/2013/jun/22/falling-short-writers-reflect-failure.

2. Anne Enright, "Falling Short: Seven Writers Reflect on Failure," *The Guardian*, June 22, 2013, http://m.guardian.co.uk/books/2013/jun/22/falling-short-writers-reflect-failure.

3. Will Self, "Falling Short: Seven Writers Reflect on Failure," *The Guardian*, June 22, 2013, http://m.guardian.co.uk/books/2013/jun/22/falling-short-writers-reflect-failure.

4. Thomas Fensch, editor, *Conversations with James Thurber* (Jackson, MS: University Press of Mississippi, 1989), 61.

5. Kristin Bair O'Keeffe, "Writerhead," KristinBairOKeeffe.com, September 19, 2013, http://www.kristinbairokeeffe.com/

6. Will Self, ibid.

7. James Rubert, "Focus On Freedom: Q&A with Author James Rubert," SimplyFaithful.com, July 30, 2012, http://simplyfaithful.com/2012/07/30/focus-on-freedom-qa-with-author-james-rubart/.

8. Lawrence Block, *Writing the Novel: From Plot to Print* (Cincinnati: Writer's Digest Books, 1985), 3.

9. Ernest Hemingway, *A Moveable Feast: The Restored Edition* (New York: Scribner, 2009), 22.

10. Diogenes Brito, "Fear of the Blank Page," Uxdiogenes.com, March 10, 2013, http://uxdiogenes.com/blog/fear-of-the-blank-page.

11. Barbara Rogan, *Suspicion* (New York: Simon & Shuster, 1999), Kindle edition.

12. Robert McKee, *Story: Style, Structure, Substance, and the Principles of Screenwriting* (New York: HarperCollins, 1997), 419.

13. Michele Weldon, *Writing to Save Your Life: How to Honor Your*

Story Through Journaling (Center City, MN: Hazelden, 2001), 23-24.

14. William Zinsser, *The Writer Who Stayed* (Philadelphia: Paul Dry Books, 2012), 4.

15. Sarah Callender, "A Conversation with ... Kristin Bair O'Keeffe," emailed article from writerunboxed@writerunboxed.com, "Subject: Writer Inboxed: We Eat Fear," September 4, 2013.

16. Kristin Bair O'Keeffe, "I Eat Fear," KristinBairOKeeffe.com, January 3, 2013, http://www.kristinbairokeeffe.com/2013/01/03/i-eat-fear/.

17. Ibid.

Fear No. 8
"I'm Afraid I Might Succeed"

———

"Procrastination is the fear of success."
Denis Waitley

———

Albert Camus was an Algerian-born French author of novels (*The Plague*), plays (*The State of Siege*), stories, and essays. Camus contracted tuberculosis in his twenties, and suffered from the disease throughout his life. He also suffered financial struggles throughout his career. His financial woes ended abruptly in 1957. To Camus, however, success was the worst thing that could happen to him.

Success came to Camus during the height of the Algerian War of Independence against France. Camus was a pacifist who believed the Algerian French (the *pied-noirs*) and the Algerian Arabs could live side by side. In interviews and newspaper columns, he advocated a truce to prevent civilian loss of life, but both the French government and the Arab rebels rejected any talk of peace.

Meanwhile, in Stockholm, the Nobel committee met to consider awarding the prizes for 1957. The committee, which has a long history of using the Nobel Prize to make political

125

statements and impact events, decided to award the prize for literature to Camus. By awarding the Nobel prize to a pacifist Frenchman from Algeria, the committee was expressing its condemnation of France's role in the Algerian War.

Camus lived in Paris at the time. He was in a café, having lunch with an American editor of *Vogue,* when a messenger handed him a telegram informing him he had won the Nobel Prize for literature. The editor, Patricia Blake, recalled that after Camus received the news, he appeared to be suffocating.[1]

The Nobel Prize for literature is the greatest honor a writer could receive — yet it was the last thing Camus wanted. He later told a friend, "I'm castrated!"[2] He saw the award as a terrifying burden, and he confided to a fellow writer, "The Nobel gave me the sudden feeling of being old."[3]

Camus wanted to refuse the Nobel, and he said publicly that his friend and fellow novelist André Malraux was more deserving. But the honor was non-transferable. The committee had made its choice. Camus felt trapped. He also needed the money, which was the equivalent of about a million dollars in today's terms. So he reluctantly accepted the prize —

And as he feared, it nearly ruined him as a writer.

At that time, Camus had already spent three years writing a play, *The Possessed,* adapted from the Dostoyevsky novel of the same name. After winning the Nobel Prize, Camus found he could no longer write — a case of writer's block that went on for months.

What caused the block? Perhaps it was the fact that he no longer felt the need to struggle artistically and commercially. He may have felt he had reached the pinnacle of his career, and no longer needed to prove himself. Or perhaps it was the glare of the spotlight that blocked him. He may have felt that the whole world was watching him and waiting for his next play — and he didn't know if his next play could meet Nobelsized expectations.

The psychological reasons for his block are unknown. We only know that it lasted for months, and he finally succeeded in completing the play in 1959, after a long dry spell.

On January 4, 1960, a few months after the play was published, Camus rode in a car with his friend and publisher, Michel Gallimard. As they passed through the tiny French village of Villeblevin, Gallimard lost control of the car. It crashed into a tree, killing both men. Camus was only forty-six years old.

Albert Camus feared the fame and financial success the Nobel Prize brought him — and with good reason. The award blocked his creativity and nearly kept him from finishing his final play.

The fear of success is much more common than most of us realize. You might be afflicted with this fear and not even know it. And it could be keeping you from achieving your goals and dreams as a writer.

Shoot for the Moon

The fear of success is the most paradoxical of all fears. Nobody consciously wants to fail. We all want to succeed — yet many of us *fear* success as much as we *want* it. Why would anyone fear success? Answer: For the struggling writer, success is the great unknown.

We ask: Will success change my life? Will I have to do media interviews? Will success disrupt my comfortable life? What if I achieve my goals only to find I'm still dissatisfied with my life? What if I find out I'm a "one-hit wonder" and can't sustain my success over the long haul? What if success makes me lose my edge and my motivation? It's easier to hide at my keyboard, pretending to be a writer, than to actually achieve literary success.

Erica Jong, author of *Fear of Flying*, says that one of the greatest fears she had to overcome was the fear of the change that comes with being a successful writer: "I have accepted fear as a part of life, specifically the fear of change, the fear of the unknown. I have gone ahead despite the pounding in the heart that says: Turn back, turn back; you'll die if you venture too far."[4]

You may tell yourself, "I don't deserve to be successful. Literary success is reserved for those *other* people, the bright and talented glitterati, the authors I see on the *New York Times* bestseller list. Those people are *special*. They're not like me."

Actually, those people are *exactly* like you. They don't intrinsically deserve success any more than you do. They've built their careers by doing the things a writer must do to be successful.

Even highly acclaimed novelists struggle with the feeling that failure is more comfortable than success. Anne Enright put it this way:

> I have no problem with failure — it is success that makes me sad. Failure is easy. I do it every day, I have been doing it for years. I have thrown out more sentences than I ever kept, I have dumped months of work, I have wasted whole years writing the wrong things for the wrong people. ... I am more comfortable with the personal feeling that is failure than with the exposure of success. I say this even though I am, Lord knows, ambitious and grabby.[5]

Those who fear success often settle for second-rate goals. They shield themselves against disappointment by setting their sights low and pretending not to care about becoming a writer.

Don't cheat yourself. Don't settle for second-rate dreams. Remember the challenging words of Charles Bukowski: "If you're going to try writing, go all the way. Otherwise, don't even start."

How big should your literary dreams be? How high is the sky? Goethe said, "He who does not expect a million readers should not write a line."

If you set high goals, if you dream extreme dreams, you might fail. There are no guarantees in the writing life. But if you're afraid to chase your dreams, you're *guaranteed* to fail. You'll doom yourself to a lifetime of regret, never knowing what you might have achieved if not for your fear of success.

Don't let fear determine your destiny. Dream your extreme dreams, then chase those dreams with everything you've got. "Shoot for the moon," said motivational speaker Les Brown. "Even if you miss, you'll land among the stars."

Here are some practical suggestions to liberate you from the fear of success:

1. Take stock of your fears.

Fear of success can undermine our goals and dreams. Instead of finishing that novel and sending it to an agent or editor, we tinker and obsess over it. We're unwilling to let it go because it might change our lives. We daydream of fame and fortune, but never get around to imposing deadlines on our dreams. Fearing success, we settle for chronic fear, failure, and pessimism.

If you are held back by the fear of success, take stock of your attitudes and behavior. Ask yourself:

• What am I afraid of? What scares me about success?

• Why am I more comfortable with mediocrity than with success?

• In what ways have I sabotaged my success in the past? How can I avoid sabotaging myself in the future?

• If I were to succeed, what would success look like? How

would my life change? How would it be better? How would it be worse?

• Do I feel I don't deserve to be successful? If so, why do I deserve to fail?

• Am I confident and do I maintain a positive attitude? Or am I always beating myself down? What can I do to become a more positive, confident writer?

• What steps can I take to ensure my continued success?

• What goals and deadlines can I set for myself?

Answer these questions honestly, then act on them. Find out what scares you, then lay that fear to rest. Figure out how you have sabotaged yourself in the past, then build strategies for success. Envision an exciting future for yourself. Imagine it, dream big dreams, and make that your vision for the future. Set goals and deadlines to motivate you toward that future.

Accountability is a powerful motivator. Ask someone you trust, someone who supports your dream of being a writer, to hold you accountable for setting goals and meeting your self-imposed deadlines. Then start making progress toward your dreams and goals.

2. Put an end to excuses.

Most writers are unaware of the many excuses they make (and yes, I've made plenty of these same excuses myself from time to time). Let's see if any of these rationalizations sound familiar to you:

"I'd like to work on my novel, but I'm too busy right now. I'll write when I have more time."

"I know I said I'd work on my novel this weekend — but what's the use? What are the odds of getting a novel published these days?"

"I should be working on my novel, but it's been a rough week, I'm tired, and I've earned this nap."

"Between traditional publishing and indie publishing, there are hundreds of new books published every week. With all that competition, why write a book no one will read?"

It's time to put an end to excuses and get serious about writing. No more procrastination, no more talking about "someday." Start writing right now.

Writing isn't a hobby. It's not a weekend project like painting the garage. It's a serious long-term commitment. You may not get to go out as much as you'd like, you may not watch as much TV as you used to, and you may not take as many naps as you'd like. But the feeling of holding a book in your hands — a book with *your* name on it — is worth the sacrifices you make.

I'm not saying you should sacrifice your marriage or your relationship with your kids. Keep your priorities straight. But if you want to be a writer, you must be willing to sacrifice your comfort, your entertainment, your sleep — and yes, your excuses.

Don't just talk about the novel you dream of writing. Make a plan and *write your novel.*

3. To stop procrastinating, set a deadline.

Fear of success makes us hesitate and procrastinate when we should be charging forward. To stop procrastinating, assign a deadline to your novel-writing dreams, just as you assign deadlines to all the other priorities in your life. Chris Baty, the founder of National Novel Writing Month (nanowrimo.org), explains:

> There's barely enough time in a day to cover all our mandatory obligations, so optional activities like novel writing, journaling, painting, or playing music — things that feel great but that no one will ever take

us to task for shirking — are invariably left for another day.

Which is how most of us become "one day" novelists. As in, "One day, I'd really like to write a novel." The problem is that that day never seems to come, and so we're stuck.[6]

Harvey Mackay, author of *Swim With the Sharks Without Being Eaten Alive*, said, "A dream is just a dream, but a goal is a dream with a plan and a deadline." To put an end to procrastination, make a plan and set a deadline. Your plan should consist of a commitment to write every day and to produce a certain number of words per day. Most full-time writers have daily word quotas of at least 2,000 words. If you are a part-time wordsmith, scale back accordingly.

One double-spaced typewritten page contains about two hundred words. If you write two hundred words a day, starting on New Year's Day, you'll have more than three hundred pages written in first draft by Halloween. That gives you all of November and December for rewrite and revision, and you will have a complete novel, ready to market, by the next New Year's Day.

Now you have a plan and a deadline. Follow the plan I just gave you, and you'll put an end to procrastination. I've done the hard part. Now all you have to do is write the book.

4. When success comes, accept it gracefully.

Sinclair Lewis was the first American novelist to be awarded the Nobel Prize for literature, which he received in 1930 at age forty-five. Lewis was known for his biting and critical view of American capitalism. He was sympathetic to socialists, Bolsheviks, and such American radical movements as the Communist Labor Party of John Reed. Though he wrote fondly of small-town America and small-town values, he often disparaged the American middle class for its "bourgeois" materialism and concern for conventional respectability.

In 1920, after a string of modestly successful novels, Sinclair Lewis published a book called *Main Street*. As soon as Lewis's agent read it, he knew it would be a hit, and he predicted it would sell at least 25,000 copies in its first year. That would have been a hugely successful book in 1920. But Lewis's agent wasn't optimistic enough. Within six months of its release, *Main Street* had sold 180,000 copies. Within a few years, it had sold an unprecedented two million copies.

Everyone was happy for Sinclair Lewis *except* the author himself. Lewis was horrified. He felt he had betrayed his leftist values by writing a commercially successful book. His biographer, Richard R. Lingeman, explained:

> The door of fame had swung open, but Lewis told some Washington acquaintances ... that he feared success: "This will change us. This will change me. This will change everything!"
>
> The Bolshevik in him worried that there was something suspect in his book appealing to so many Americans. He told [novelist Joseph] Hergesheimer he had heard that "some bunch of the very young jeunes — say, those at the Café Rotonde on the Rive Gauche — assert that if the damned book has sold so well, I must be rotten. But I agree with them, I belonged to their faction! Hell's sweet bells, here is divine comedy! An earnest young man ... writes a long book to slap the bourgeois — [and] the bourgeois love it, eat it!"[7]

The very people Sinclair Lewis lampooned in his books — the materialistic middle class — *loved* his book and *bought* his

133

book. They made him comfortably wealthy. And that's why he despised his own success.

According to one account, Lewis was once accosted by a matronly woman a few months after the release of *Main Street*. She was bedecked in jewels, and Lewis could see that she was a typical representative of the bourgeois class he so deeply despised. She gushed with praise for his latest novel, and Lewis couldn't stand it. He interrupted her and told her to go straight to blazes.[8]

If you happen to write a million-seller, I hope you'll accept your success with better grace than Sinclair Lewis. Use your fame and your wealth wisely. Don't let it go to your head. Spend some, invest some, and share some of your good fortune with those who are less fortunate than you.

And if you still feel weighed down with guilt because you're so wealthy and successful, please write to me. I will gladly help you ease your burden.

---

1. Peter Lennon, "Camus and His Women," *The Guardian*, October 15, 1997, http://www.theguardian.com/books/1997/oct/15/biography.albertcamus; Elizabeth Hawes, *Camus: A Romance* (New York: Grove Press, 2009), 261.

2. Jay Meija, "The Short Happy Death of Albert Camus," *Literary Kicks*, November 16, 2002, http://www.litkicks.com/AlbertCamus.

3. Olivier Todd, *Albert Camus: A Life* (New York: Knopf, 1997), 381.

4. Erica Jong, *What Do Women Want? Essays by Erica Jong* (New York: Tarcher, 2007), 62.

5. Anne Enright, "Falling Short: Seven Writers Reflect on Failure," *The Guardian*, June 22, 2013, http://m.guardian.co.uk/books/2013/jun/22/falling-short-writers-reflect-failure.

6. Chris Baty, *No Plot? No Problem!: A Low-Stress, High-Velocity Guide to Writing a Novel in 30 Days* (San Francisco: Chronicle Books,

2004), 29.

7. Richard R. Lingeman, *Sinclair Lewis: Rebel from Main Street* (New York: Random House, 2002), 163.

8. Ibid., 164.

Epilogue
"Be Invincible!"

———

"Good novels are written
by people who are not frightened."
George Orwell

———

Carson McCullers was born Lula Carson Smith in Columbus, Georgia, in 1917. Her novels and stories were mostly set in the American South, and dealt with tragic themes of loneliness, spiritual emptiness, and failed love. In 1937, at age twenty, she married a promising young writer, Reeves McCullers.

Three years later, in 1940, Carson McCullers published her first novel, *The Heart Is a Lonely Hunter.* The book was a critical and commercial success for the twenty-three-year-old author. Yet, even as her career was soaring, her marriage to Reeves McCullers was failing. Carson and Reeves separated in 1940 and divorced the following year.

Carson McCullers moved to New York and joined an arts community that included W. H. Auden, Tennessee Williams, and composer Benjamin Britten. After World War II ended, she moved to Paris. There she remarried Reeves McCullers. It was a tempestuous relationship that plunged her into a deep depression. Their love was doomed by Reeves's struggle with writer's block and alcoholism, along with his jealousy over Carson's literary success.

In 1953, Reeves begged Carson to join him in a suicide pact. She refused, and fled their Paris hotel room. Reeves was found later, dead of a barbiturate overdose. Carson later wrote about her trauma-scarred marriage in her short story "Who Has Seen the Wind?" (published in the September 1956 issue of *Mademoiselle*), which she later adapted into a play, *The Square Root of Wonderful* (1957).

"Who Has Seen the Wind?" is a horror story — not a work of supernatural horror à la Stephen King or H.P. Lovecraft, but a tale of mounting fear. It's the kind of fear only writers truly understand. McCullers tells the story of a writer whose only successful novel was followed by years and years of writer's block. The story begins:

> All afternoon Ken Harris had been sitting before a blank page of the typewriter. It was winter and snowing. The snow muted traffic and the Village apartment was so quiet that the alarm clock bothered him. ...
>
> His prelunch drink (or was it an eye opener?) had been dulled by the can of chili con carne he had eaten alone in the kitchen. At four o'clock he put the clock in the clothes hamper, then returned to the typewriter. The paper was still blank and the white page blanched his spirit. Yet there was a time (how long ago?) ... when the empty page summoned and sorted memory and he felt that ghostly mastery of his art. A time, in short, when he was a writer and writing almost every day. ...
>
> Now he sat there, hunched and somehow fearful.[1]

Carson McCullers knew that fear very well. She had suffered from it herself, and she had seen how that fear had ravaged her alcoholic husband like a full-blown disease. It's the fear suffered by a writer who has lost faith in the creative process, who has forgotten how to invite the inspiration of the Muse. It's a mind-killing fear, the little death that obliterates imagination and creativity.

In her novels, stories, and stage plays, Carson McCullers wrote about the tragedies of her life. She contracted rheumatic fever when she was fifteen, suffered a series of strokes while still in her twenties, and by age thirty-one was paralyzed on the left side. In 1967, in her home in Nyack, New York, she was dictating her autobiography when she suffered a brain hemorrhage and died. McCullers was fifty years old.

In her unfinished autobiography, published decades after her death under the title *Illumination and Night Glare*, Carson McCullers confessed, "There were so many frightful times when I ... feared that I could never write again. This fear is one of the horrors of an author's life. Where does work come from? What chance, what small episode will start the chain of creation?"

She went on to talk about the story she had written about that fear, the story called "Who Has Seen the Wind?" She said, "I once wrote a story about a writer who could not write anymore, and my friend Tennessee Williams said, 'How could you dare write that story? It's the most frightening work I have ever read.'"

It is, indeed, a frightening tale. It even scared McCullers herself. She said, "I was pretty well sunk while I was writing it, and was thoroughly glad when it was finished."[2]

This fear — the fear that stalked Carson McCullers, the fear that horrified her friend Tennessee Williams and drove her husband Reeves McCullers to suicide — need not destroy you or keep you from writing. You now have the practical insights and strategies that most writers only wish they had. You now know what most writers wish they knew. You have the tools to overcome:

- The fear that you lack talent.

- The fear of the blank page.

- The fear that you cannot finish.

- The fear of risk.

- The fear of self-revelation.

- The fear of rejection.

- The fear of failure.

- The fear of success.

You know how to replace fear with courage, self-doubt with confidence, paralysis with action, and writer's block with productivity. But we're not quite done. I want to talk one more time about something we touched on in Chapters 1 and 5 — writing "in the zone."

The zone of fearlessness

A young writer recently told me she was considering independently publishing her novel. I said, "That's great. Indie publishing is a time-honored path to becoming an author. The list of indie authors includes some celebrated names — Poe, Dickens, Twain, and Walt Whitman, to name a few. So tell me — why are you choosing to go indie?"

"Traditional publishing scares me," she said. "I'm afraid of having my work judged by agents and editors."

"Well, as I said, I'm supportive of indie publishing, but I don't think you should base your decision on your fears. Make a decision based on your strengths and your courage. Indie publishing demands just as much courage of an author as traditional publishing — maybe more. It takes courage to be your own publisher, to market yourself, to go on social media and interact with your readers. If you think agents and editors are tough, wait till you see your reviews on Amazon.com! Whether you submit your work to traditional publishers or you choose to self-publish, it takes courage to be a writer."

I'm not sure if I convinced that anxious young writer that she needed to find her courage. But I hope I've convinced you.

What is the most reliable source of a writer's courage? I believe the best place to find your courage is "in the zone." In my own indie-published book *Writing in Overdrive*, I reveal practical techniques for writing "in the zone," in that amazing realm of heightened creative awareness where we tap into the unconscious mind ("the Muse"). When you write "in the zone," you feel no fear, no inhibition, no attacks from the Inner Critic. When you are writing "in the zone," you don't even notice the passage of time.

Novelist Virginia Woolf (*To the Lighthouse* and *Orlando*) knew about being "in the zone." She described the experience of creative flow as "the exalted sense of being above time and death which comes from being in a writing mood."[3] Similarly, John Gardner referred to the "in the zone" state as "the fictive dream," explaining:

> In the writing state — the state of inspiration — the fictive dream springs up fully alive: the writer forgets the words he has written on the page and sees, instead, his characters moving around their rooms. ... The dream is as alive and compelling as one's dreams at night. ... [The writer] sees made-up people doing

things — sees them clearly — and in the act of wondering what they will do next he sees what they will do next, and all this he writes down in the best, most accurate words he can find.[4]

Once you've entered "the zone," you'll finally know what it means to write without fear, without anxiety, without self-doubt. Experience it once, and you'll want to go there again and again. And the good news is that you *can* go there, practically at will. All you need is an understanding of the creative process and how you can tap into the power of the unconscious mind.

Lest you think that this epilogue is merely a commercial for *Writing in Overdrive*, let me suggest another book that can also help you write "in the zone." Whether or not you read *Writing in Overdrive*, you owe it to yourself to read Dorothea Brande's *Becoming a Writer*, originally published in 1934 and still in print today. The writing principles she offers are timeless and her book will help you to write "in the zone."

One of Brande's best-known pupils was Ray Bradbury. He discovered her book when he was eighteen years old and he lived by its principles throughout his adult life. Bradbury's biographer, Sam Weller, wrote about the one and only fear that haunted the author of *The Martian Chronicles* and *Fahrenheit 451* during his writing career:

Ray Bradbury lived his life in a race against time. He had so many things to do and to say, and he felt he did not have enough time in which to accomplish them all. Perhaps that was why he so often wrote of time machines. With devices to travel back to the past and forward to the future, he was able to right the wrongs of yesteryear and to prevent the seemingly inevitable mistakes of tomorrow. To Ray, time represented mortality, an end to his creative output. He did not fear death itself; instead, he was frightened of being unable to write. And so Ray Bradbury wrote as if he were making up for tomorrow's lost time.[5]

One of the ways Ray Bradbury made up for lost time was by writing quickly, under the influence of the Muse, totally unthinking and completely dependent on his unconscious mind. For years he kept a sign beside his typewriter that read, "Don't Think!" Bradbury believed conscious thought to be the enemy of creativity. He believed that the only good writing is fast writing. "In quickness is truth," he said in a 1987 essay. "The more swiftly you write, the more honest you are. In hesitation is thought. In delay comes the effort for a style, instead of leaping upon truth."[6]

So, whether you choose to read Dorothea Brande's classic *Becoming a Writer* or my book *Writing in Overdrive* (or both), I urge you to discover the freedom of writing fearlessly "in the zone." Experience that realm of creativity where there is no self-doubt, no self-criticism, no anxiety, and no fear. In "the zone," there's timeless joy, uninhibited spontaneity, complete relaxation, intense focus, and utter fearlessness.

When you write "in the zone," you are invincible.

Write fearlessly and change the world

One of the most fearless writers who ever lived was a teenage girl, Anne Frank. She preserved her wise and beautiful thoughts in a diary she received on her thirteenth birthday. While hiding with her family in some hidden rooms in a house in Amsterdam, she chronicled her life from June 12, 1942 until August 1, 1944. It was the time of the Holocaust, and Anne Frank was Jewish.

An informer betrayed the Frank family to the Nazis, and

Anne and her family were arrested on August 4, 1944. Anne died at the Bergen-Belsen concentration camp in early March 1945, just a few weeks before the camp was liberated by the Allies. She was fifteen years old, and died never knowing the enormous impact her diary would one day have on the world.

While writing her diary, Anne dreamed of becoming an author. Her dream was realized when her diary was published in 1947. Here is a brief passage from *The Diary of a Young Girl*:

> I'm overjoyed that at least I can write. And if I don't have the talent to write books or newspaper articles, I can always write for myself. But I want to achieve more than that. I can't imagine having to live like Mother, Mrs. van Daan and all the women who go about their work and are then forgotten. I need to have something besides a husband and children to devote myself to! I don't want to have lived in vain like most people. I want to be useful or bring enjoyment to all people, even those I've never met. I want to go on living even after my death! And that's why I'm so grateful to God for having given me this gift, which I can use to develop myself and to express all that's inside me![7]

Does Anne Frank speak for you? Do you want to go on living, even after your death, through this God-given gift, through your ability to write? Then take a page from Anne Frank's diary and write fearlessly. Let me suggest a few ways you can embolden yourself to write fearlessly:

• Study the lives of successful writers, learn about the struggles and obstacles they overcame — and the fears they conquered — to achieve their dreams.

• Attend writers' workshops, conferences, and classes to

sharpen your skills, build your confidence, and connect with publishing professionals and fellow writers.

• Join a writer's group. Connect with other writers who are serious about their craft.

• Learn to view every challenge as a voyage of discovery; transform fear into excitement.

• Let go of perfectionism. Don't worry and obsess over what editors and readers may think. As you write, have fun! Creativity should be joyful, exciting, and exuberant. Shed your inhibitions, become a child again, and *just write*.

• Above all, write freely, write quickly, and write daily. It's paradoxical but true: The best antidote to the fear of writing is *writing*. The more you write, the less you fear.

• Finally, keep your fears in perspective. Ask yourself, "What am I so afraid of?" Are you afraid you can't start, you won't finish, or you might fail?

What if being a writer could get you killed? Have you ever risked your life to write? Would you dare to write if the stakes were that high?

Malala Yousafzai is a Pashtun school girl from Mingora in the Swat District of northwestern Pakistan. Her name, Malala, means "afflicted by grief," and she is named after Malalai of Maiwand, a Pashtun warrior-poetess who fought against the British in 1880.

From the Swat Valley, where the Taliban had forbidden girls to attend school, Malala blogged on a BBC website, writing about life under Taliban oppression and about her dream of being educated and living free. After the *New York Times* produced a documentary about her life, Malala gained worldwide fame. She gave media interviews and won countless new readers to her blog.

On October 9, 2012, Malala and her classmates took exams at school and were returning home aboard a makeshift schoolbus — an open-back truck with benches for seats and plastic sheeting for windows. A Taliban assassination squad halted the vehicle and a masked gunman stepped aboard and shouted, "Which one of you is Malala?" The gunman chose his target and began shooting, hitting Malala and two other girls. One bullet hit Malala in the forehead, went down her neck, and lodged in her shoulder.

All three girls survived, though Malala was comatose and in critical condition. After Pakistani doctors stabilized Malala, they airlifted her to Queen Elizabeth Hospital in Birmingham, England, for surgery and intensive rehabilitation. She was released in January 2013, but returned in February for a five-hour operation to reconstruct her skull and restore lost hearing in one ear.

On her sixteenth birthday, July 12, 2013, Malala addressed the United Nations in New York. "Dear friends," she said, "on the ninth of October 2012, the Taliban shot me on the left side of my forehead. They shot my friends too. They thought that the bullets would silence us, but they failed. ... I am the same Malala. My ambitions are the same. My hopes are the same. And my dreams are the same.

"Dear sisters and brothers, I am not against anyone. ... I do not even hate the Talib who shot me. ... This is the forgiveness that I have learned from my father and from my mother. This is what my soul is telling me: be peaceful and love everyone.

"The extremists are afraid of books and pens. The power of education frightens them. They are afraid of women. The power of the voice of women frightens them. ... There was a boy in our school who was asked by a journalist, 'Why are the Taliban against education?' He answered very simply by pointing to his book. He said, 'A Talib doesn't know what is written inside this book.' ...

"Let us wage a glorious struggle against illiteracy, poverty and terrorism. Let us pick up our books and our pens. They are the most powerful weapons. One child, one teacher, one book, and one pen can change the world."[8]

A Taliban bullet could not intimidate this young writer. In the face of terrorist threats, she remains fearless.

How does your courage stack up against that of Malala Yousafzai? Do your fears prevent you from writing? If a terrorist's bullet can't silence this school girl, how can you let the fear of the blank page or the fear of rejection silence you?

To be a writer is to suffer fear — but great writers are not ruled by their fears. They are driven by their passions and led by their courage.

So live courageously. Write fearlessly. Be invincible.

Change the world.

———

Are you in earnest? Seize this very minute;
What you can do, or dream you can, begin it.
Boldness has genius, power, and magic in it.
Only engage, and then the mind grows heated.
Begin, and then the work will be completed.
Johann Wolfgang von Goethe[9]

———

1. Carson McCullers *Collected Stories of Carson McCullers* (New York: Houghton Mifflin Harcourt, 1998), 171.

2. Carson McCullers, edited by Carlos L. Dews, *Illumination and Night Glare: The Unfinished Autobiography of Carson McCullers* (Madison: University of Wisconsin Press, 2001), 37.

3. Sharon Klayman Farber, *Hungry for Ecstasy: Trauma, the Brain, and the Influence of the Sixties* (Lanham, MD: Rowman & Littlefield, 2013), 298.

4. Adrienne Miller, *Esquire's Big Book of Great Writing: More Than 70 Years of Celebrated Journalism* (New York: Hearst Books, 2003), 315.

5. Sam Weller, *The Bradbury Chronicles* (New York: Morrow, 2005), 183.

6. Ibid., 205.

7. Anne Frank, *The Diary of a Young Girl* (New York: Knopf, 2010), 204.

8. Becky Bratu, "'I Want to Tell My Story': Malala Yousafzai Memoir to Be Published This Fall," NBC News, March 27, 2013, http://worldnews.nbcnews.com/_news/2013/03/27/17490294-i-want-to-tell-my-story-malala-yousafzai-memoir-to-be-published-this-fall?lite; Ian Johnston, "Malala Yousafzai: Being Shot by Taliban Made Me Stronger," NBC News, July 12, 2013, http://worldnews.nbcnews.com/_news/2013/07/12/19432997-malala-yousafzai-being-shot-by-taliban-made-me-stronger?lite.

9. Ralph Waldo Trine, *In Tune with the Infinite* (Radford, VA: Wilder Publications, 2007), 103.

Recommended Reading

As Dorothea Brande said near the end of *Becoming a Writer*, "Now read all the technical books on the writing of fiction that you can find. You are at last in a position to have them do you some good." Here are some books I recommend:

Chris Baty, *No Plot? No Problem!: A Low-Stress, High-Velocity Guide to Writing a Novel in 30 Days*
Chris Baty is the founder of National Novel Writing Month (NaNoWriMo). In this book, he reveals the secrets of writing and finishing a novel in thirty days.

James Scott Bell, *The Art of War for Writers*
Best-selling suspense novelist James Scott Bell gives you a strategy for winning the internal and external battles of creating characters, plotting stories, querying and submitting, and overcoming rejection and self-doubt.

James Scott Bell, *Plot & Structure*
Award-winning author James Scott Bell shows you how to craft strong stories, brainstorm original ideas, and correct common plot problems

James Scott Bell, *Revision & Self-Editing*
Take your first draft from "so-so" to "sold"! James Scott Bell shows you how to transform a fast first draft into a fine-tuned manuscript agents and editors will fight for.

Lawrence Block, *Telling Lies for Fun and Profit*
Edgar Award-winning novelist Lawrence Block's classic book on writing fiction gives you the tools to master the techniques, skills, tools, and disciplines of a published writer.

Ray Bradbury, *Zen in the Art of Writing*
"*Zen in the Art of Writing* is purely and simply Bradbury's love song to his craft." —*Los Angeles Times*

Dorothea Brande, *Becoming a Writer*
This classic work explores the power of the unconscious mind to help you become the writer you've always wanted to be.

Terry Brooks, *Sometimes the Magic Works: Lessons from a Writing Life*
New York Times bestselling author Terry Brooks shares his secrets for creating powerful, memorable fiction.

Jonathan R. Eller, *Becoming Ray Bradbury*
Though this book is primarily a biography of one of America's favorite authors, Eller also reveals many of the secrets to Bradbury's approach to the craft of writing.

James N. Frey, *How to Write a Damn Good Novel*
Written in a clear, understandable style, this international bestseller is a crash course in the essential techniques of novel writing and storytelling.

John Gardner, *The Art of Fiction: Notes on Craft for Young Writers*
This classic guide to the craft of fiction continues to inspire generations of aspiring writers.

John Gardner, *On Becoming a Novelist*
With humor and style, Gardner reveals the joys and challenges of the writer's life, discussing issues ranging from dealing with editors and agents to an exploration of the creative process.

Jeff Gerke, *Plot Versus Character: A Balanced Approach to Writing Great Fiction*
What's more important to a story: a gripping plot or compelling characters? This hands-on guide to creating a well-rounded novel embraces both crucial story components.

Stephen King, *On Writing: A Memoir of the Craft*
Equal parts autobiography and writer's workshop, written by a bestselling master of the writer's craft.

Anne Lamott, *Bird by Bird: Some Instructions on Writing and Life*
Lamott offers a wise and witty take on the reality of the writer's life.

Madeleine L'Engle, *Walking on Water: Reflections on Faith and Art*
The author of *A Wrinkle in Time* shares her insights into the nature and purpose of writing, art, and faith.

Donald Maass, *Writing the Breakout Novel*
Renowned author and literary agent Donald Maass teaches you how to take your writing to the next level, both artistically and commercially.

Donald Maass, *Writing 21st Century Fiction*
Using thought-provoking prompts and examples from best-selling novels, Donald Maass gives you the tools you need to create fiction for today's generation of readers.

Steven Pressfield, *The War of Art: Break Through the Blocks and Win Your Inner Creative Battles*
Conquer the enemy of your creativity and success—an enemy known as Resistance.

Sol Stein, *How to Grow a Novel: The Most Common Mistakes Writers Make and How to Overcome Them*
Stein, the author of nine novels and the editor for such luminaries as James Baldwin, Jack Higgins, and W. H. Auden, reveals the secrets to creating gripping plots and unforgettable characters.

Sol Stein, *Stein on Writing*
Stein himself explains, "This is not a book of theory. It is a book of usable solutions—how to fix writing that is flawed, how to improve writing that is good, how to create interesting writing in the first place."

Sam Weller, *The Bradbury Chronicles*
More than a biography of Ray Bradbury, this book reveals the sources of Bradbury's creative genius. An inspirational, motivational resource for writers.

Sam Weller, *Listen to the Echoes: The Ray Bradbury Interviews*
Fascinating interviews with the leading proponent of writing "in the zone." Interviews are arranged by topics: childhood, Hollywood, famous friends, faith, art and literature, writing and creativity, sexuality, politics, and more.

Recommended Writing Software

Dragon NaturallySpeaking speech recognition software for PC.

Dragon Dictate, Version 3.0 speech recognition software for Mac.

Dr. Wicked's Write or Die writers' productivity software.

Scrivener software for writers. Outline, edit, storyboard, *write*. See Scrivener in action and download a free trial. Or download **Scrivener For Windows** or **Scrivener 2 for Mac OS X** at Amazon.com.

"Proceed with confidence, generating it,
if necessary, by pure willpower."

William Zinsser

From the Same Author:

WRITING IN OVERDRIVE
Write Faster. Write Freely.
Write Brilliantly.
by
Jim Denney

"If my doctor told me I had only six minutes to live,
I wouldn't brood. I'd type a little faster."

Isaac Asimov

Author Jim Denney is a veteran of both traditional and indie publishing. He has more than a hundred published books to his credit, including the Timebenders science-fantasy series for young readers. In *Writing in Overdrive*, he shows you how to:

- Write so fast you'll have no time for self-doubt.
- Set ambitious yet attainable productivity goals.
- Overcome self-defeating habits and inner resistance.
- Tap into the power of writing "in the zone."
- Use powerful "writing rituals" to prepare yourself to write.
- Become undistractible—even amid distractions.
- Leverage the motivational energy of NaNoWriMo.
- Eliminate writer's block, and MORE.

Available in Trade Paperback ($8.99) and
Kindle Edition ($3.99) at **Amazon.com**.

Coming Soon

MUSE OF FIRE
Ninety Days of Inspiration for Writers
by
Jim Denney

"O for a Muse of fire, that would ascend
The brightest heaven of invention!"

William Shakespeare,
Prologue to *Henry V*

Do you struggle with procrastination and a lack of inspiration? Are you often defeated by an inner resistance to a daily writing habit? Then you'll want to read *Muse of Fire*, ninety daily entries designed to get you fired up and inspired to write. Each entry contains motivational stories, quotations, and insights designed to get you "in the zone" and on your way, your writer's soul ablaze with energy and ideas. Dwell in this book for ninety days and be empowered to achieve your creative goals and dreams.

63556403R00087

Made in the USA
Lexington, KY
11 May 2017